The Facts & Lies
and then Ignore

Youngsoo Youn

The Facts & Lies and then Ignore

Written by Youngsoo Youn

Published by Haedream

jlee5059@hanmail.net

3-4, Gyeongin-ro 82-gil, Yeongdeungpo-gu,

Seoul, 07371, Republic of Korea

TEL : 82-2-2612-5552

FAX : 82-2-2688-5568

1st Printed, September, 1, 2024

First Published, 2024

ISBN 979-11-5634-595-4

Preface

There are works and workplaces of adults all in the world.

Most of them will repeatedly be doing their works which were started from the beginning until retirements.

Some of them work with emotionless machineries. These people don't need to be agonized or suffered from stress. There are no other desirable lives if there are no insufficient things in their life-styles.

We can find something in common they have in their lives. They are not to obsess outcome and profits, and tactlessness and simple-minded. They are also resolve problems by fair means and positive thoughts, but they have a strong sense of identity.

People want to live comfortable lives without exception reaching old ages for the rest of their lives. But, there would be some cases to be circumstantially delayed as the personal situations may be.

However, there was a person who should unfortunately be in crisis of dishonorable retirement by an absolute unwillingness in the meantime his retirement date was set up due to meet a very bad other party.

He visited anywhere everybody believed to, but he got a nasty insult instead of removal of his disgrace from there. Finally he appealed that he should relying on where he was sure to be helped, but he received a clear message that couldn't help him in there.

Now he takes off the disgrace and insult by himself, and will quietly be living rest of his life after retirement while appreciates all of them whom gave an opportunity of such a thing.

Contents

1. Preface — 3
2. The First Chapter — 7
   The First & Lies and then Ignore
   1) Report of Operation — 8
   2) Additional Evidences — 9
   3) Letter to Refree — 13
   4) Second Additional Evidences — 17
   5) PETITION — 20
   6) The Fact & Email — 53
   7) Petition of Appeal — 57
   8) Last Evidence — 59
   9) Vividly Fixed Evidence — 73
   10) PETITION 2 — 75
3. The Second Chapter — 81
   Criminal prosecution request letter to lawyer
4. Epilogue — 107

The First Chapter

The Facts & Lies and then Ignore

- This chapter is a 'compliation' of only the documents submitted to the court and emails exchanged with the court during the 1 year and 9 months of Disputes Tribunal trial.

- To help Viewers understand, the Writer's Commentary' and some deleted parts have been inserted and written in '**Gothic**' font.

- The parts marked 'Highlight' in this chapter are about 'specific global advertising media.'

- Some parts have been deleted or omitted from the documents submitted to the court, but no parts have been modified.

- The displayed case number, person's name, company name.. etc. are different from reality.

Report of Freezing System Operation
Meadowban BP Station

Date   25 November 2021

Time   3:00pm ~ 7:48pm

I had Refrigeration Equipment installed and have it reached to target temprature -20°C reaching at 7:48pm after doing operation of cooling down by on order of you.

I was wondering following problems happened on system controlling during this work process.

Abnormal phenomena along with this type of problem Result are;

1) After defrost terminating, cond. unit must run with Freeger fan running simultaneously.
   (Cond. unit was running over 10 minutes with Freeger fan no running even through it not allowed for a second.)

2) Recovering time back to normal temp. previously like after defrost termination is delayed over 30 minutes rather then restarting in a few minutes.

3) The most important is becoming cause of compressor demage because liquid suction to compressor directly occurred without evaporation.

Thus problem solving is;

If a specialist who handles "ir 96 controller of CAREL" product could simply solve this matter within a few minutes with button controll to the experienced understanding.

Electrical Service Technician: EST243006   Youngsoo Youn

Additional Evidences of the Claim / CIV-2021-055-000   / Youn v Wu

The Claim evidences of mine to make up for as follows;

23/11/2021 around 4pm   (My work finished 2 days ago)

    The day I work in the gas station I purposely called out Wu's couple who were outside by cell phone, and I would be replacing new unit which was on my burden of $3000 worth on condition of removal of another cond unit already done.

    We got a mutual agreement as below;

1) Paying immediately the balance $4360.00 by transfer when Freezer Room temperature reaches -20°C.

2) I provide Cond Unit Cover Drawing and Wu's responsibilities are her payment & set up.

25/11/2021 at 7.52pm   (The day I finished my work)

    I sent her a photo of -20°C Freezer Room image by text.

    *This meant my work was completed perfectly. *

    So, I requested her to pay the balance immediately, but she broke her promise.

28/11/2021 at 9.43am   (3 days later she broke her promise)

    I sent her Operation Report by email. I did let her know causing problem & result in the report. Solving it I obviously made a sure that problem of the system was not my responsibility. And then I requested her fulfilment of the promise(payment) again.

    Same day at 12:00 noon

I explained Cause & Result of the Controller problem in front of the controller face to face in detail, directly visiting her workplace. And I repeatedly requested to fulfill her promise to pay. However, she had her husband not to pay the balance while he was showing aggressive attitude in argument with big tone each other. Finally I explained at the scene my intention rely on appealing to the law, and I left their workplace.

Above First Claim

Following is Wu's improper status record which Xue Wu selected from her submitted counter claim file. This is specified as an evidence in my second claim.

25/11/2021 – My work was completed perfectly   (C1A3)

      Freezer Room reached -20°C

      * Wu broke the promise.*   (C1A3)

26/11/2021 – Next day Wu broke the promise

      After then Wu ordered Condensing Unit Cover Processing and paid   (C2A3-3)

      At that time I thought Wu confirmed my work was completed.

(At this time, the cover processing fee given by Wu was $287.50. However, in the 'Order' issued 371 days from that date, it is ordered that "Youn must pay Wu $287.50 for the condensing unit cover fee.")

29/11/2021 – Wu sent me an email:

      Wu wrote the other story only except essential point which she broke the promise.   (C1A6)

30/11/2021 – Email Wu sent me;

      Again she told the background of the story except the essential fact she broke the promise. She commented at end part of the email, "Now I will ask a Refrigeration Company to get an Inspection and Report."   (C1A7)

01/12/2021 – I, Youngsoo Youn, submitted First Claim by online.

04/12/2021 – She made a fake Inspection Report calling out an unqualified person. (C2A3)

*(At this time, Wu's cost of making the 'fake report' was $375.75. The 'Order' from court issued 363 days later states,
"Youn must pay Wu $375.75 for the report one.")*

07/12/2021 – Wu sent me a Black Email as follows;   (C2A3-2)

      "Due date 5pm Sunday 12/12/2021, Take your Condensing Unit and Inside Cooler Unit away and then immediately refund $4,000.00 when you take a way your Unit."

(At this time, the $4,000 extortion money requested by Wu was issued 360 days later, and in the 'Order', it was ordered that "Youn must pay a refund of $4,000.")

08/12/2021 – After sending me a Black Email previous day, at 5pm she texted me, "I sent you an email yesterday. Please check it. Please let me know if you didn't receive it."

So, I emailed to Wu like below;

"I had completed the work in my responsibility complying with contents of our contract as dropping to -20°C promised temperature on 25th November 2021, 7:48pm, after finishing my work all in duty.

And I emailed her 'Report of Freezing System Operation, in which problem solution method in detail. On same day I explained letting you know face to face the problem in detail, visiting directly your workplace.

However, you refused to pay the balance $4360.00 while did not do anything to solve the problem on your duty at all to keep doing wrongful behavior intending not to pay it afterwards, either.

'The equipment which was not paid the balance was not yours.' You must know you can not use the facilities or touch them without doing your job on duty for problem solving as I pointed out already.

"I am notifying you Xue Wu is accused of the same above to DISTRIBUTE TRIBUNAL COURT filing on 1st December 2021."

10/12/2021 – For all that Wu picked up Cond Unit Cover.   (C2A3-3)

Wu did self-proven by this fact that she was cheating .

12/01/2022 – (2 days prior to submitting her Counter Claim)

Wu got a Quotation of total amount of $11,551.75 from P-company.

Cond Unit capacity of '54LZBIN' which marked on the quotation could cover twice of Wu's Freezer Room space.

It was impossible to install Evaporator AL26 Unit cooler's Fanx2 (currently Fanx1) in Wu's F/R crawl space.

There is no reason to replace the equipment nor could doing like above.

Wu unbelievably submitted claim amount which was inflated increasingly like above to Court 2 days later.

14/01/2022 – Same day, Wu submitted a Counter Claim of $13,339.00 against me to Court.

16/02/2022 – Wu was impudently attending at First Hearing teleconference where she told the story, I was guessing over a half an hour, in which exactly same as before. That was to say she insisted her absurd past story except the key point she broke the promise.

(Following the 'bad relationship' with Wu, who was born with 'bad karma', at the first hearing held two months and 15 days after I filed with the court, another 'terrible bad relationship' was waiting for me. The bad relationship began with the first words of Hearing's progress statement, and she appears to have received and written the letter I sent 46 days after that day, and executed it 243 days after that. Now, another 7 months have passed since then, and this is the whole reason why I had no choice but to write this book.)

18/02/2022 – Wu emailed Court, "I really need to install the new equipment." and "as early as possible.", she did push next Hearing.

// Correct and Repeat of mistyping of Second Claim file //

Part 4: Detail of dispute

(Attachment 3-3) end part: that Sue Wu → that Xue Wu

(Attachment 6) 2nd paragraph from the end: Young Soon Youn's → Young Soo Youn's

Letter to Refree

Dear Sir/Madam

I am applicant Youngsoo Youn, case number CIV-2021-055-000

I carefully read the Counter claim of respondent Xue Wu

I will be re-responding against her aggressive counter claim as follows;

1. Let me explain her bad behavior I was refraining from mentioning so far because I expected her behavior to be corrected by herself with conscience. Also, because it was nothing to do with this case.

2. As applicant position, I will be explaining the hearing which was held on last 16th February 2022.

3. Let me explain how much Xue Wu's bad behavior seriously was affect my business.

Please understand me sending this postal letter to you personally, because I thought above my 3 explanations were inappropriate at formal process of court room. Appreciate that.

○ Explanation of Xue Wu Counter claim

1/1-1 Wu (The main problem is Youngsoo installed the wrong condensing unit.)

First of all, let me abridge words to be understood well.

- Compressor + Condenser = Condensing Unit = Cond. U/T
- Compressor = Comp. = Heat Pump
- Comp. Capacity = Nominal Horse Power = HP
- For Medium Temperature = For MT
- For Low Temperature = For LT

As part of Global Warming Prevention MT and LT were divided since launching of New Refrigerant which was developed for the purpose of Energy saving.

So, LT Comp. is small size (1/3 HP ~ 3 HP) limited to Hermetic reciprocating type, and use range is also limited to small storage of Room temp. -20°C frozen food in which fluctuating load is small, too.

For your information, one MP comp. covers before GWP or Use range -25°C ~ -16°C (Freezer), 0°C ~ -6°C (Fridge) in Domestic Refrigerator (below 1/3 HP).

This means all Comp. designs are always standard Max. Load Condition, and there is a limitation of power saving.

Mechanical principle of LT Comp. is an occurring structure to save power when it's running on motor rotation motion for reducing heat, involving lots of laminated steels of stator and reducing number & length of insulated coating huge lengths copper coil.

Thus, Hermetic steel housing dimension is the same as Comp discharge rate, but weight is lighter & price is cheaper than.

Price difference of Cond.U/T including Cond. Is swell. Because MT Cond. Heat Exchange Coil surface is taking over. This real one of Cond. U/T is currently on roof top of the Petrol Station. Subsequently Xue Wu has illegally been distraint above all over 4 months.

For your information, I will be showing AW43M and AW43L in comparison. (Wu submits evidence highlight.)

43 MT   2HP   69kg

43 LT   1-1/4HP   60kg

Difference between LT Comp. and MT Comp.;

MT Comp. is much better than LT Comp. because it is in higher efficiency on condition of LT as well as using as many for, while LT Comp is used on condition of LT only that never used on condition of MT.

Then, why? There could be a question that why the expensive one was replaced even free of charge service. The answer is that 3 major supply companies is reluctant to import it due to fewer demand here and there is no stock.

Above explanation tells Xue Wu was intend to leave $4,360.00 unpaid which was over 1/2 of total counter claim amount $8,360.00 (equivalent US$3000). Moreover, she did counter claim of $13,339.00 which was over 3 times of the balance. Consequently above facts all was proved as fraudulence.

1/1-2   Wu (whatever qualification or license he has.)

Sending my Certificate & Performance chart to Wu was making sure her my qualification. However she didn't stop her bad behavior, and was even mocking me. I am sure someday she would be in big repentance.

As a result, there is no reason for replacing, couldn't do and would not be in the same service. Xue Wu is probably an idiot or patient or evil nature because she has continuously been kept persisting its replacing.

II. On 16th February 2022

Teleconference Hearing on that day began about 15 minutes late and ended 15 minutes earlier than schedule without any information in advance, and subsequently couldn't understand the tribunal situation of the critical issue. At last I realized the translator's ability & skill are affect the applicant and dependent importantly. Then I was afraid that this dispute could be on mediation or negotiation in mood of demoralization.

However, the atmosphere on that day stimulated me to prepare Additional Evidences further, and I submitted them to Court while Wu was in high spirits encouraged from last teleconference positive mood for herself with self-confidence.

Anyway I am satisfied I am able to explain the background like this.

One thing I hope is Wu's false claim & unusual behavior were made clear caused by my additional evidences. So I expect no more next Hearing preparation is needed that means it would be end last teleconference.

*(In the first hearing 46 days ago, this very 'II' devoted more than three times as much speaking rights to Wu, while the irregular proceedings that reduced my speaking time were euphemistically compared to an interpreter who was significantly different from the actual interpreter of the other party. I believe that what was expressed provided an 'excuse for reversal.' In particular, I believe that the two-character Korean word 'conscience' mentioned to Wu in 'I' acted as a catalyst, and 'An Unwanted Order' was issued on December 2nd of the same year.
And even though it was a small claims dispute trial under $30,000, I believe that the 'incomprehensibly long gap' in which the second and final hearing was held a whopping 9 months and 16 days after that date is also closely related to this letter.)*

III. According to Googl Bid Statistics for last 2 years and a half, average impression share chart is obviously on the top ranking. At this point rival companies put the blame on me as unfair.

However, I am not profit seeking enterprise but just a self-handling business for a living. If I am running with recruit employees in technical superiority for pursuit of profits the rivals' saying is right as disturbing market order. But I have never been done like that so far.

Moreover, everybody knows the issue in relation with Xue Wu in this dispute. I know well they all desire I would be disappeared from their market through this tribunal dispute. Even if Judgement comes out of Wu's 100% fault I would be gotten a blow inevitably. I think it's my fate.

I have been struggling continuously in very uneasy relationship with Googl advertising medium.

Whenever staff on changed I have a Zoom meeting with Googl Ads, and I have been requesting correction of the ad system repeatedly but there was no answer even I repeatedly sent emails 27 times totally.

I recently became aware of it why there was no answer. Because they on behalf of rival companies holding in check of my overwhelmingly ranking on top. Therefore I sent an email Googl. with a reasonable solution plan last January.

The point I expecting is that the result of judgement would be positive influence on that part. It would be appreciated if you carefully refer to this attachment which is closely connected with Wu.

Please excuse me if I were straightforward and rude expression on this letter.

Highly appreciated your kindest reading long story of this dispute.

Very kind regards

Applicant Young Soo Youn

2nd Additional Evidences of the Claim / CIV-2021-055-000 / Youn v Wu

Dear Sir/Madam

1. 1 December 2021

    Applicant I, Young Soo YOUN, filed court documents to Disputes Tribunal against Wu who didn't pay a balance $4,360.00 breaking her promise

2. 14 January 2022

    Respondent Xue WU submitted a fake document of counter claiming for $13,339.00 over 3 times her balance to court in collusion with an unqualified person Amar in which she created some reasons regardless of breaking promise above mentioned absolutely.

3. 2 February 2022

    I submitted 1st additional Evidences to court in which I refuted WU's absurd insistence, but the document was returned in any doubtful reason.

4. 16 February 2022   <1st Hearing>

    WU took up her time 3 times than me at the 1st hearing to conceal the fact of her breaking promise above mentioned and rationalize her deceiving behavior in justification of it.

5. 21 February 2022

    I re-submitted the 1st Additional Evidences to Court.

6. 1 April 2022

    WU submitted a reference doc which demonstrates hot main issue as 'wrong Condensing Unit' to court while she did counterclaim with 3 times of it following not paying her original balance because of YOUN's responsibility as well as his mistake, putting the blame on.

    Evidential material was the E-mail in which WU's conspirator Amar and sales person Dan were corresponding. Dan is a Sales person belongs to Supplier company for 15 years well known by myself, too. The date was shown on 30 March 2022, a day before submitting it to court.

7. 11 April 2022

    I posted below written contents enclosing to Referee.

1) Explained WU's bad behavior
2) Explained the 1st Hearing
3) Explained my business was affected by WU's bad behavior

Please understand me my sending this postal letter to you personally, because I thought above explanations of 1), 2) & 3) were maybe inappropriate at court room in formal process. And I explained the difference between MT Condensing Unit and LT Condensing Unit. As a result, those were explanations that Wu and Aman͵s intentional false claim was wrong.

8. 12 May 2022

   I received an E-mail from Court that 2nd Hearing would be held on 8th July 2022.

9. 2 June 2022

   WU sent me my Operation Report which I wrote Mett in Whit. Ref. by E-mail. I was very glad to receive it. Because I thought she was doing to keep her original promise after realizing henceforth what's wrong with her, since there was a way for problem solving to solve the problem of WU's Freezer Room simply in the Report. And also because the couple of WU's bad behavior so far just started from then, too.
   Because it was natural that No 1 Refrigeration Service company in NZ experienced for 50 years traditionally should know the controller problem as the couple also knows it well.

10. 7 June 2022

    At sight of the 'Condition Report' of Whit Refrigeration which WU submitted to court I couldn't be doubtful my eyes.
    *Picture 1: Evidence photo WU submitted to Court on 4 January 2022
    *Picture 2: Black Cable Tie left side means it was damaged since then. Even though there was Galvanized Steel Cover, the Terminal Box should be covered by vinyl-guarded rapping. Water drop mark on Steel Cover right side was showing the photo was right at that time, but I am doubtful that why she should closeup the point area particularly by way of excuse Rust.
    *Picture 3: It is nothing to do with the issue.
    *Picture 4: It is Switch of Chiller Cond. Unit which is the same type wrapped around Black Tie left side.

*Picture 5: This is the picture closed-up of Photo 1.

*Picture 6: This is the photo I sent to WU by Cell phone which I asked her to make a Steel cover by herself when I completed the installation.

*Picture 8: This photo was not need to be taken because the report said "This is may not be up to code."

All of above pictures were focused on some desperate reason of WU's surroundings suspiciously as I think by inference. It is possible that "WU would be giving all when she get $13,000 after trial." if she promised. Basis of the inference was that parts all needed to be replaced in the context of the report, especially explicit at Pic 7 in the beginning, and gradually faded away for pretending it's normal.

I think we have to understand it's difficult time to be endured to so much big company these days.

However, this model company in this country made a mistake of definite technical error which must not be happened as 50 years experienced traditionally in the field of Refrigeration Service. I was wondering why Whit Refrigeration did so, if they didn't know or pretending ignorance or ignoring me. It was clear that Wu's couple plainly knew the situation in fact.

In Controller Section of 10-20 WU was concentrating attack as main point on me on title of Top page 4 a) & b), just using this paragraph "The Controller is functional and faults were found." In other words, Whit Refrigeration was thoroughly exploited by WU, I dare say. I will be informing you of this related story in which disclose WU's identity in next section describing in detail.

11. I have been lived here in NZ for 20 years and 6 months as Refrigeration Repair Serviceman only in life.

    I have happily been worked with only this job thoroughly because I was in position as carrying out following 3 principles in my occupation.

    1) I don't do any work needed anybody else' assistance.

    2) I absolutely do not receive a charge of money until completing the work.

    3) I do not do any work needed taking time over one day.

Generally the work of 80% was firstly filtering on the phone, and the rest of them were settled onsite secondly.

(Hereinafter, the 14-page manuscript is omitted from the 2nd additional evidence of the claim.)

PETITION

Dear Sir/Madam,

Re. CIV-2021-055-000   Youn V Wu

I explained below contents as a petition in which I submitted on Tuesday.

1) The fact that Xue Wu made bad use of my Service.

2) The fact that Anan orchestrated Wu's wicked act.

3) The fact that documents submitted to Court were forged by Whit & Pete Pen Refrigeration.

4) <mark>The fact that Googl Ads team continuously harassed advertiser with irrelevant unfair way in systematically.</mark>

I tried to prove above 4 facts.

I am additionally submitting those by USB to make up for more visually.

Applicant Youngsoo Youn

Dear Sir/Madam

I had done a sue Xue Wu for a Disputes Tribunal matter filing on 1 December 2021. But this dispute was not terminated while 2nd Hearing was scheduled on 21 October 2022.

My business should be closed in unavoidable situation of mine myself regardless of this dispute on 31 March 2022, but I have been running my business while I encountered Wu involved this matter in.

I faced the financial difficulties at the moment after then as follows;

*Credit cards of 2 banks of mine were exceeded Advance limitation.

*Three times overdraft facility after extension once of my main bank

*I have barely managed to get along on private loan & other from one of only two friends of mine so far, but there is no way to get along anymore from now on.

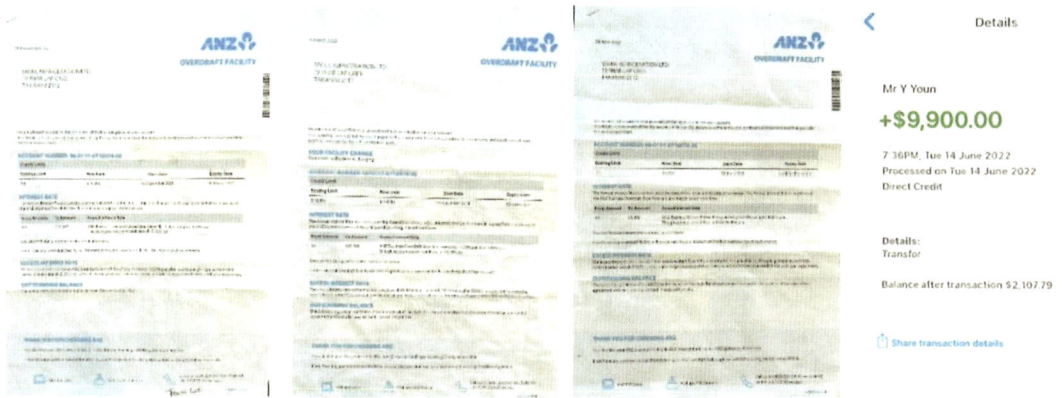

Those financial pressure made me to ready for submission of 3rd Evidences which were technical and psychological proofs renewably in after 2nd evidences of postal submission on 5 July 2022. However, I must explain and prove the 3rd evidences with inappropriate and unfair things of Ads team of the global enterprise 'G' in absurd ways which were destined to meet wicked Wu inevitably. Thus I will be explaining the Team with WU in detail.

I am raising this petition, expecting upcoming 2nd Hearing completed as final course at Distributes Tribunal and final ruling hopefully.

Xue   Wu

1) Wu's Refrigeration Electricity Equipment of the gas station was originally constructed by unqualified person without planner design, and also it was unauthorized Equipment unable to get Electricity Safety Inspection.

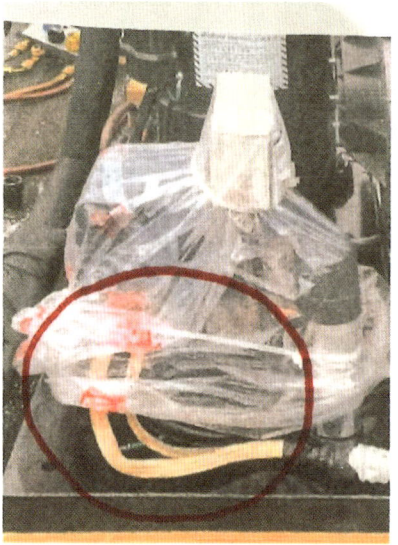 

Electrical wire of the emphasized part must not be exposed to outside, and it is connected to power point of the wall through Elect. Steel Pipe laid already into the bldg. concrete. I Electrical Service Technician also cannot treat This Elec. Wire. It is handling by Electrician only. If I explain Wu's Electricity Equipment easily in comparison with the joint area of power point socket and refrigerator flexible lead cord plug meet, without the met area non flexible hard copper Elec. Wire is unable to be connected to control board of Refrigerator. That meant qualified designer who knew Electricity Act & Regulation well would not work like this, and moreover EST or Electrician knows importance of the regulation wouldn't do the work like this through onsite work. Those pictures are at 1), 2) of Top page as the most important issue in the Whit   Report which were wrote for evidences Wu submitted on 4 January 2022.   After 140 days Whit   Refrigeration reused 6/9 of the evidences which were submitted on 4 Jan 2022 by Wu, and wrote for the court submission on 24 May 2022.

2) Wu's Freezer Equipment has not been operated for a long time. The first day, after carrying on Cond. Unit to the roof I checked Unit Cooler by Install manual in advance. I found there was no rotation of Unit Cooler Fan while hearing Motor run sound when I checked it in advance by Install manual after cooler power switching on. At last I had it operated after hand turning over 10 times manually with inserting a driver between Grills after switching off. After then I felt a resistance feeling on hand grabbed driver in noisy 'gigigick'. The noise came out from time to time after switch turning on. Later I explained Wu the reason of replacing Unit. Cooler, the interval noise to her. It is common with F. company product most widely supplied here, in case of old model Refrigerator Fan 60x1.5watts if it were reusing after left in garage 1-2 years it happened occasionally, but tipping something to the part makes it running normally. However, Wu's Freezer Room 300x90watts Axial motor case could not estimate as it never happened before.

3) Much water fell over the electrician soaked through Elec. Pipe while working when Wu's partner also confirmed physically, it was usual case, being caused by removing Freezer Equip not operated long time.
If it has been running until recently one of 3 young man part timers entering the room of Wu's gas station was maybe a victim of electric shock. It would be happened a disaster around there caused by fire related to Elec leakage because Wu's gas station was treating & storage of the first rank dangerous place.

4) I had ever explained that there was no need Freezer room at gas/fuel station at 13/18 page of 2nd Additional Evidence submission to court by postal on 5 July 2022. There would not be like WU's Freezer Room of the gas station at anywhere in this country. If it was anywhere the equipment were already removed or would be left unattended without using even left somewhere.

5) WU saw my Ad while her Cond. unit out of order already and a no running Unit. Cooler were left unattended, and she seemed to be paying attention on "No charge No Fix" of my Ad. She was probably thought the best chance she could save much money without deposit for Cond. Unit replacement even though she had her unnecessary Freezer equipment keeping then. Because it is commonsense every installation work must be deposited to worker by 1/2 of all costs before starting the work, and more cost must be burdened to user in case of additional work

needed out of the initial quotation. (Refer to bellow Quote)   I draw attention it was the fact that WU knew the Unit Cooler problem in advance. And I raised this issue as first topic when I called up WU's couple and was promised bank transfer immediately after reaching -20°C.

6) Wu called 'P' Refrigeration for Cond. Unit quotation only to carry out her plan Quote of $7785.00+GST, and just before a day she approached me. Thereabout my business situation was that I decided to close my business effective from 31 March next year. Abnormal positioning of my Ad by Ads team has continuously been done. In the event of normal Ad positioning in November beginning of peak season could cover 3-4 real work, but the day WU rang me was 3rd day morning I had nothing to work for 2 days.

On the phone I instingtively felt to say 'No' to her of work asking. However, I was not in a position then in my difficult financial status to wait for customers or choose the job.

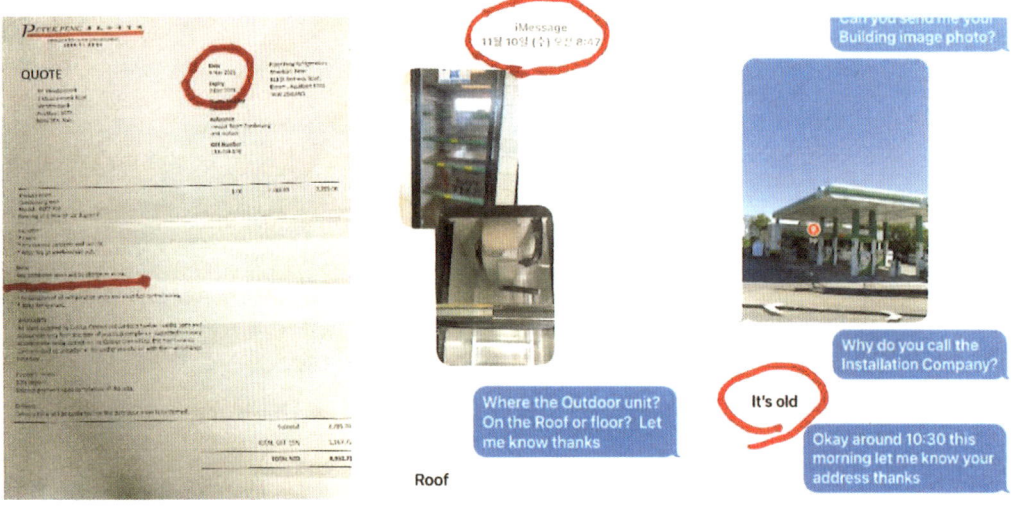

Through her text messages I became aware of her suspicious lie, but I made an appointment to see her for confirmation of her intention. When I got the onsite a middle aged man only was there while she sent me onsite photos dodged the place. The man told me she was owner.

7) I confirmed a Compressor dead caused by Valve plate broken, checking Condensing Unit on the roof.   Only the person who experienced to cut open steel housing for finding cause of dead could know it. Anyway after confirmation of

(This part proves that even back then, the root cause of the accident was a broken controller.)

same model stock was at supplier's. And I rang WU to recognize who was the man at her counter, and she answered me he was her husband. After confirmation of the man's existence, I texted her an estimate to leave basis behind.

8) Estimate comparison

	P company	me
Price	$7785.00	$4600.00
Worker(s) number	3x2 days	1x6 hours
Carrying on the roof	Crane only	Truck driver helpx20min
Ordinary Profit	Total amount x 30%	0

*The reason why my ordinary profit '0' for, I don't do pursuit of profits.

9) My 2nd Additional Evidences

Refer to <11 November 2021> & <12 November 2021>

10) Unusual Ad positioning, broken promise, of the Ads team made me to meet Wu the worst money player inevitably. I had been working for 17 days to complete the work anyhow even though 6 hours enough on my effort in normal case due to geting out of WU's evil playing.

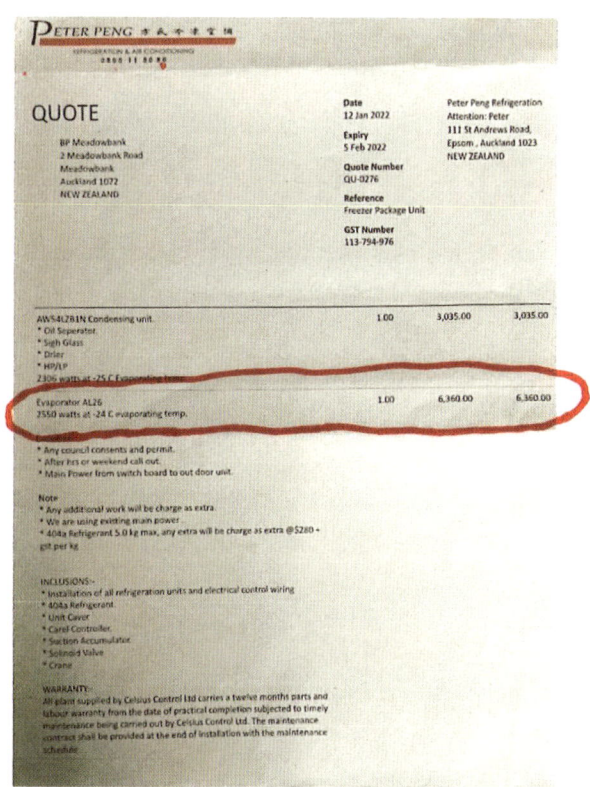

According to the Quote of 'P' Refrigeration cooperative to WU's purpose to submit Court it was $6,360.00 for Evaporator(Unit cooler) replacement work, while I did $1,800.00+GST actual supply price of Unit cooler only.

Finally I knew the fact that all problem of the system were in Controller.

When I visited supplier's to buy same model to replaced it, but I was unable to have it because the part was already discontinued model 20 years ago.

(Refer to 2nd Evidence Att 5)

In last way I took a consideration of stepping up Cond. Unit capacity. If did so I calculated trouble holding up time about 16 hours as well as time shortening to reach -20°C with upgrade of Cond. Unit capacity. Of course, it was unnecessary work if I purchase the same model of the controller.

I called up Wu and her partner onsite, and I got they promised that balance bank transfer would be done immediately after reaching -20°C.

11) Next day, after installation of new Cond. Unit I did Pressure test – Vacuum test – Refrigerant change completion while I was up and down roof & freezer room over 10 times. When I leave the room after last checking of Freezer Room I instinctively felt something strange on that, as slimly expected a very thin sound of Refrigerant gas leaking came out of outside of 150mm Sandwich Insulation Panel at Freezer room ceiling.

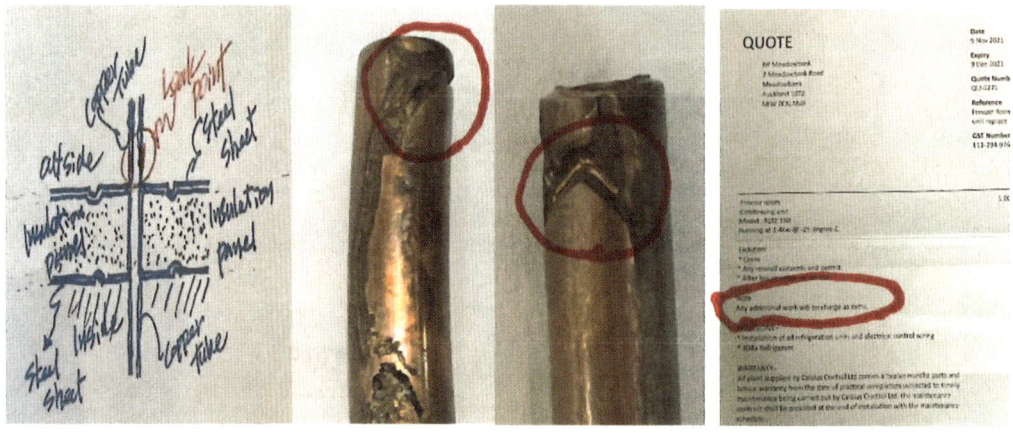

It is the worst work in basic skill job to prick hole with drilling and push up from lower part of Cupper pipe torn into and also pulling down from the roof repeatedly. The workers involved in Wu's wildcat scheme were unprofessional as well as pursuing money only same as Wu.

Worker cannot approach to the leaking area because of narrow space. At last after detaching that area I replaced a new copper tube working over 3 hours completely, and showed the detached part piece to WU. She looked it away after having it a look once as if 'why are you show me such a piece? What do you want should I do? I could take a consideration of balance payment or not paying after seeing reach-20°C' This also WU should get burden of herself 100% if she put deposit 1/2 of the whole payment before starting the work. And she should promise to additional payment over $2,500.00 for EST time charge + Waisted R404a Refrigerant immediately. If not, work stopped and she must give up the deposit. And moreover, if the worker claims indemnity for that WU's loss would be rising because it's not user's right only.

12) Refer to 2nd Additional Evidences / 25 November 2021

13) It was Sunday 8:00am in the morning when I sent my Report to WU. I thought the day WU's couple would turn up even though their off day. Because I believed they would pay the balance if they saw the report which got a solution of the matter. In the report I wrote concerned Controller trouble and influence to system by it's failure at the end of it. ('ir 96 controller of CAREL' product could simply solve this matter). This meant there were significant number of normal controller left at other gas stations because they were unnecessary in BP Headquarter I guessed. Reviewing a variety of Wu couple's suspicious attitude & acts she seemed to ready 2nd plan for welching the balance after 1st plan to solve the controller problem without paying by herself anymore cost. That is to say, she didn't need to be in a hurry to solve the trouble as far as she confirmed reaching -20°C. And also she could do any action on that referring to my Report any time. As a result she conspired the balance $4,600.00 became her own wholesome.

14) Wu conducted 2nd plan action like evil after passing the deadline of her 1st plan, expecting I would come again onsite. From then no license holder Anan who was

irresponsible to Wu sank deeper into the pit entangled, manipulating documents all submit to Court led by himself.

15) On 7th day of starting WU's plan she sent me a Blackmail. (2nd Evidences Att7)

'Withdraw all equipment you installed by 5:00pm in 5 days, and refund $4,000.00 you got received already as interim.', sent me like this in midnight. If I were such a worker they thought the worker must give up the money facing the horrible blackmail. That day Wu did bad act which crossed a line of moral justice of humanity. She didn't realize that I lodged a court file against her.

16) Wu submitted counter claim document of claiming 3 times as much as the balance a month before Hearing with manipulated documents. Such her behavior met the result of impure intent of the Ads team had been planned long time ago.

It was a starting point to be effective of the result. Following is her key counter claim amount $13,339.00 she created in cooperation with 'P' Refrigeration.

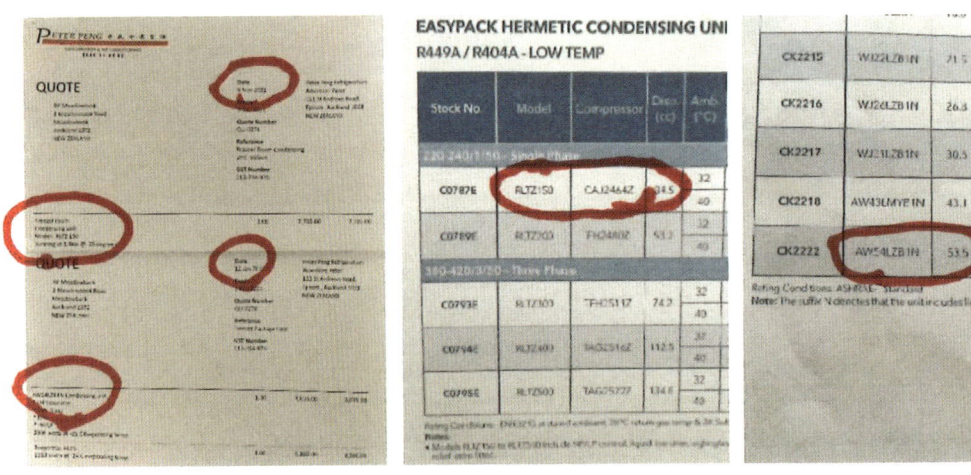

Every accurate capacity of compressor is calculated by discharging gas volume.

    9 Nov 2021   RLTE 150   34.5cc

    12 Jan 2022   AW54LZBIN   53.5cc

*It was exaggerated by 55% raising 2 steps.
*There was 2x300Fan of Evaporator AL26. Currently 1 Fan narrowly put into WU's Freezer room. So, how could put Evaporator sized twice in there? Why this fact took place? 'P' company and WU could know the fact well.

17) Worker receives relevant wage after completion of the work user requested. There is no worker to request money without completion of the work. If there are such a

worker the person should be terminated worker's life. If both parties were face to face at 1st Court Hearing I might suggested WU, "I will forget the balance $4,360.00, and give up your counter claim $13,339.00!" Because there were no need mediation and agreement between WU and me on this matter. However, this matter went well because I could disclose the Ads team's disgusting conduct in the mammoth global 'G' enterprise.

18) Then Wu was a heroine who could terminate my business life on behalf of all of Appliance maker, Supplier and Repair Service companies at once. This was due to that the team was giving strong message behand every day.

19) Trac Cui, a friend of Wu's, posted a malicious comment on my Business Review. (2nd Evidences Att 8)   I could realize that the profile team as well as the Ads team took part in knocking my business Seoul Refrigeration off due to this negative comment.

20) The manipulated document Wu made it a month prior to scheduled 2nd Hearing is the best Report of 'W' Refrigeration amongst all of forged documents.

① Report is made by like unqualified Wu's boyfriend Anan , or it should

not be written without mentioning trouble part originally.

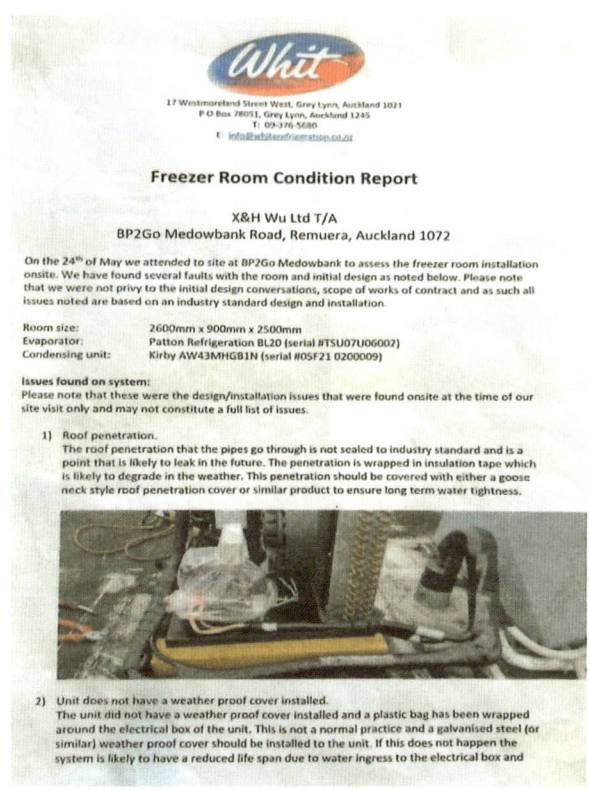

By the way, in 'W' company Report they wrote absolutely different issue as the first priority on Top of the front page. It was suspicious 'W' company went to onsite of the place in advance because the photo Wu provided was attached in fact.

② "No faults were found" wrote in Controller about column 20) of 'W' company Report. Wu had truly been heroine role to the end while attacking me lastly on behalf of all companies at that. Reviewing my Report, Wu and Anan had this issue deepen to welch $4,360.00 expecting they would not to see me anymore because I completed my job over there. Didn't 'W' company know that? Didn't they see my Report? This is the same as family doctor submits a forged Death Report as Alive Report to the court.

Like this 'Mineend named Train of Xue Wu' is riding toward Destruction terminus continuously.

*Mistyped words were corrected in the court submitted documents. *

The Ads Team

1) I was Chief Engineer & Owner of Refrigeration Plant Engineering company in Seoul, South Korea till just before immigrating to New Zealand. Motive of immigration to here is to concentrate living with my family until my life ending in selecting this city of a good environment country such as advanced education for my children, mild temperature not extremely hot in summer time and cold in winter...etc. I had running a limited company in a building only one place without any advertising medium using or without just a salesperson employing for 13 years there.

2) In January 2002, upon arrival here in NZ my alone business had been advertised through Korean restaurants, grocery shops and others of wide Auckland area for 2 years, and Advertisement fee was about 3% of monthly Sales amount. 2 years later I had community magazine Ad stopped, and started to advertise to Central, East & South Auckland except North & West Auckland through Classified of Local Newspaper. Subsequently I have financially been lived enough with my family for 13 years even though Sales decreased much with around 5% of Ad expenses in comparison monthly sales. However, after then Sales had gradually been diminished and I had been opening an account of Googl Ads eventually.

3) Relationship with the Ads Team had been started from April 2019, beginning of 5 months normally advertised on Top page of Ad section with Ad expenses doubled over. Monthly Sales didn't make no difference then in comparison with previously for 13 years, so I made a hopeful future plan which I could help neighbors needed. But when passing 5 months my Ad was abnormally kept positioning in the back page here and there. That is to say, for instance, Call-out request came from far away over 20km or company name only showing at Ad title, or telephone number only appeared at the section absolute different from initially promise. In other words, I couldn't understand there were no principle and criteria of positioning on that as well as broken promise. Of course, my sales were diminished by 30-40%.

4) In 2 months doing so, there was first video meeting with the Ads 'A' senior staff. In the meeting he answered me, "it would be a certain time taken" as convey to Headquarter as Ad positioning concerned I raised. But it never been corrected going by 6 months after then. Of course I had been sending claim mail him 6 times, but never responded from anybody. After again 6 months later, 2nd video call conference with the 'A' senior staff was held. I brought up the same issue, and he added "I promise Top page positioning but it's hard to put it on Top of the front page." So, I asked him "Could I contact you if this promise were broken?" and he answered "Yes". However, the promise was also broken. So, I emailed him twice to keep the promise in 2 days and 5 days later. But he has never responded me so far.

I really didn't understand him because I was sure he would be a reliable person to keep his promise then. This is another story personally. I can figure out any person who he is through conversation a little differently from others. In this respect I've got big help for social life of mine. Accordingly it is my greatest asset for me.

5) At this point I thought if I have Ad time adjusted they would probably normalize my Ad positioning to fulfill the budget. And I accessed processing of Ads manager mode -> Key word -> Set. But "You already did adjustment of the time, so you are unable to adjust it again anymore" popped up on screen absurdly. At this time I firstly realized I was being under special restriction. So, I decided to treat time adjustment with Budget increasing together while waiting for change of duty staff.

6) I got a video call conference with 'S' senior staff after 'A' 2 months later. He seemed

a reliable person genuinely with kindness like 'A'. I wanted to increase my budget by 35%, and time adjusted diminishing from previously 12 hours to 8 hours. Then he had Max. Cpc bid limitation increased by 72%, but it was on precondition of Top page promise. So, there was no way to agree with the measure in my position. And normal positioning was maintained for 22 days but returned to abnormal statue again. Again I emailed him to urge to fulfill the promise twice. Subsequently it seemed to be normalized for 20 days.

7) One day I got a phone call from 'S' senior staff, he said "Change your Translator" to me then on the phone. Changing my translator meant his dangerous suggestion to fire my essential staff like pressured on me. I felt his voice was trembling when he added last comment "This is just for you." On driving I suspiciously thought for a moment that there may be responsible for all these abnormalities to upper management than 'A' previously or currently 'S' so far.

8) Immediately after, I found an astonishing fact.

I am layman of computer and, moreover, I am not interested in statistics. I saw an unbelievable Graph when I accessed to summary of Manager mode in cursor movement firstly, and when I put key word 'Bid Statistics' I had a look a Chart, too.

9) In those days I found another statistics which is absolutely not suit to me as well as nonsense of basis of the calculation.

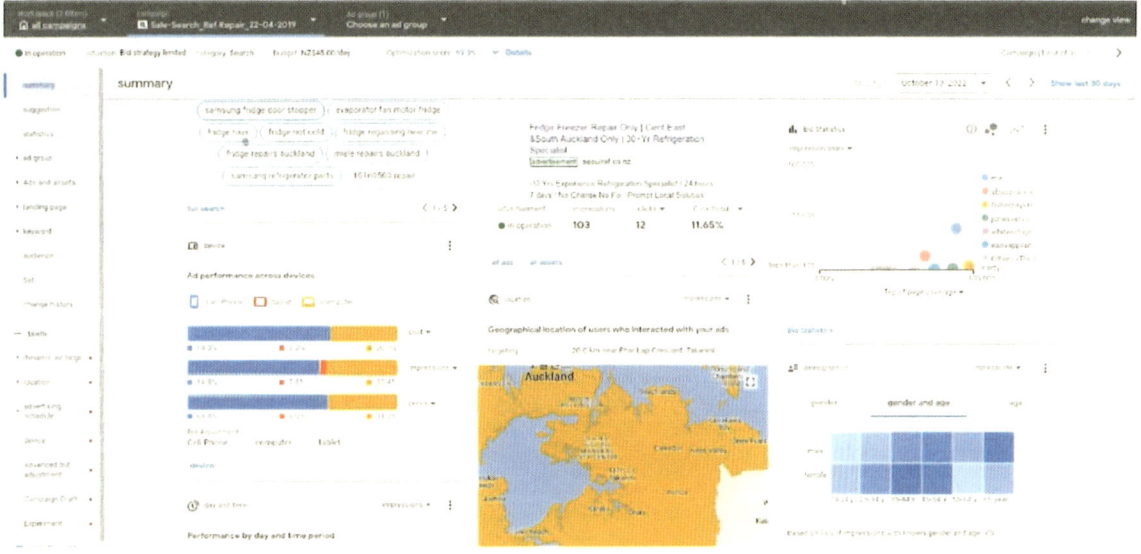

On the day I never did real work except 1 phone call for washing machine from out of 20km North and 1 phone call for dryer from out of 20km at West. They know these phenomena. If anybody enlarged it on the spot he or she could understand those immediately. Nevertheless, Click numbers were full on that day. For more information, they have been withdrawn fully monthly fee all from my bank account except 1 month for self-rest and 2 months for accident treatment.

10) In those days, I found a signal like medal on me my company amongst the numerous companies.

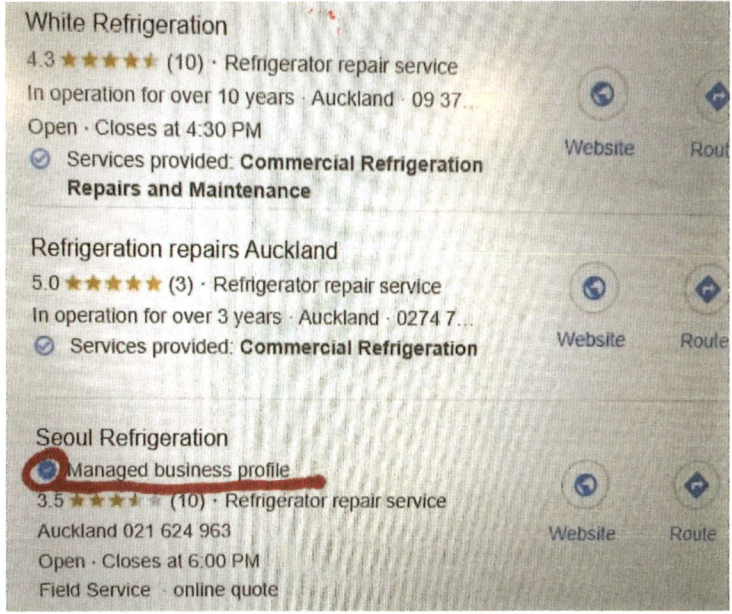

This is a message to other companies that they will certainly have my company broken up soon. I am sure this message correspondence of the Ads Team between

'P' company and 'W' company which helped Wu was done reckless deed.

11) I will be interim breaking up 3), 4), 5), 6), 7), 8), 9) and 10) except 1) & 2). The team should do solve this matter reasonably from the beginning as chances were a few times to solve this problem on the way. But they were hoisted with their petard while they would like to kick out me easily. Anyway they had been done to turn me, one person company in small & old, out from this field market viciously from the beginning 2 years ago. With abnormal positioning and statistics tool they sent mails to relevant companies regarding my personal business alone should be closed itself blocking its income. Even though their maneuver was successful it was early to forejudge the result. At that time it was 2 months ago entering into our bad relationship with Xui Wu.

12) I have been waiting for duty staff changing only because I knew the team's ugly intention and needed to confirm some surroundings around them. But I have never been gotten any mail from Ads team for a phone meeting the year changes. So, I sent an E-mail to senior staff 'S' currently on duty with 'Suggestion' titled and New Year greetings in January 2022.
In the suggestion, ① The reason why my Ad should be corrected to normal position.   ② The reason why my Ad needed to be excepted from the statistics.   I mentioned like this reasonably.

Lastly, I cordially requested to help me mentioning the reason why I must do work.   (Refer to Postal letter to personally on 11 April 2022, Attached Part)

13) However, the Team refused this my reasonable suggestion again. That meant 'Now if you realized this situation go out after closing your business without any reason telling.' as tacit message.

14) I've got a mail from new face 'B' junior staff regarding phone consultation meeting appointment. After 15 days again the junior staff sent me mail to urge to hold phone meeting. So, I sent her last mail in which the reason why I didn't want a phone meeting and I didn't like to beg their Ads after deciding to close my business effective on last 31 March. But, I hinted her if I got a judgement ongoing trial with bad persons I would return for I got suffered from WU through SNS, and they were also not free from blaming in the field if they do not normalize my Ad even not so long time left. Personally I have been kept any promise I made so far in my life. In fact then, I was ready to write 'Huge

mountain swallowed echo' titled in which written impact against image of Global 'G' enterprise if they did the wrong activities continuously.

15) Then a new junior staff 'V' turned up as their hackneyed staff changing card, and suggested a phone meeting. I answered 'V' that I would like to deal with 'B' only who promised 4 days ago, adding "This is for former seniors and your company." So then 'B' questioned me what I wanted. Lastly I ordered the promise made by former seniors should be kept. After then, nearly normalized my Ad positioning was kept going thanks to her anyway.

16) One day then, anybody posted a negative comment in my Business Review. I have happily been working here for 20 years, facing words of heartfelt gratitude from nearly all customers every day. By the way, recently I got 4 absurd bad comments of there for 6 months, but I disregarded them because I was going to close my business anyway. One fake negative comment among them is a friend's of WU's. (2nd Evidences Att 8) So, I asked Business Profile Team to review them, and I got replied from them to be notified the result in 3 days after receiving the mail. However, there was no news from them over for 20 days. So, I requested the junior staff 'B' to delete them urgently, but there no answer for that, either. I reminded her it again.

17) Following day senior staff 'S' appeared and he irritated me, adjusting my Ad positioning to under Washing machine Repair which was free 42nd rather than 6th of my normal position far from deleting the negative comments.

18) Unidentified strange Ads showed on Top page with 'S' senior staff's splendid appearance as follows;

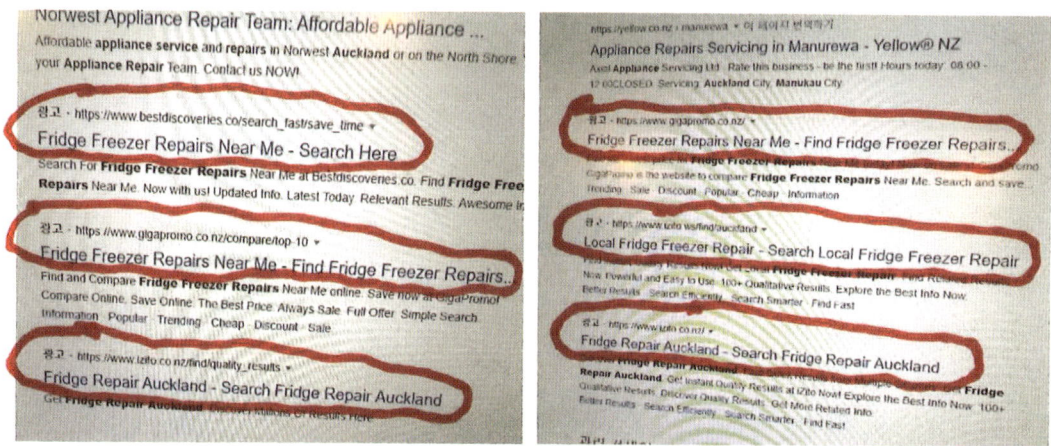

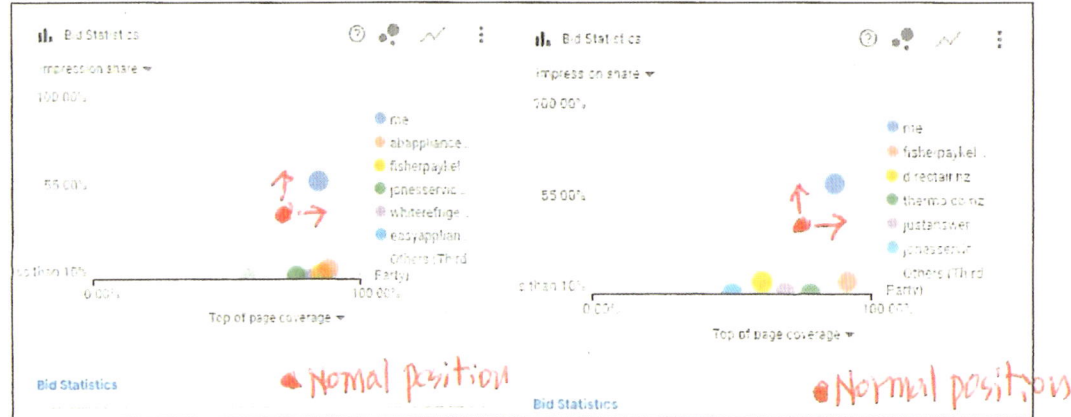

Impression share on Graph is higher than normal. Top page coverage is located to right than usual time. On this day, there is real work with no phone call without exception. Persons only who know characteristics of my Ad would be counterfeiting this technically. This is showing to get Ad fee only while they tighten my income to be zero, stimulating other companies to the end.

19) I sent him a warning E-mail in 5 days after the 'S' staff's appearance. I explained the progress going by in the meantime in detail, notifying recently mail correspondence, and lastly, I told that I wanted to finish bringing this issue with junior staff 'B' happily. This E-mail is the last warning mail. Nevertheless he continuously did the worst positioning the improper work as if he sneering me, 'What shall you do?..' At last, this case will be on the light of sunshine even though the Ads team with a project of shading spot designing has been attempted to defoliate me alone company for 3 years more or less.

20) I gave up my simple dream so far, and decided to be buried beside my mother who passed away in her life of 100 years four years ago after quiet living but this complicated saga is challenging me. Anyway, I will be return for those issues entangled to them. I am sorry to whom responsible all and their families, Junior staff helpful especially, and I would like to say goodbye all.

*Following is the ultimatum E-mail to senior staff 'S' *

보낸 사람: 윤 영수
보낸 날짜: 2022년 9월 25일 일요일 오후 12:41
받는 사람: kokkiligad　@googl..com
제목: FW: Letter from Youn (Seoul Refrigeration)

Dear Bharga

Please refer the below email sent to Sharu

Kind regards

Young Soo Youn / Seoul Refrigeration

보낸 사람: 윤 영수
보낸 날짜: 2022년 9월 25일 일요일 오후 12:28
받는 사람: sharukhkh　@googl.com
제목: Letter from Youn (Seoul Refrigeration)

Hello Sharu　,

Thank you for your email which is a catalyst to be cleared strained relations between you and me while I am about to leave Googl Ads.

First of all, I would like to retrospect about 'my ad positioning' which was just one issue I have been raised complaints for around 3 years numerously.
The reason why my ad title 'Fridge Freezer Repair Only' is I can repair Refrigerator only among Appliances. Other Refrigeration product (eg. heat pump, cool room...etc) work needed assistant manpower or ladder using. Namely, I do not work alone myself any job over 2 hours taken or danger of accident.
I've never been worked except once. (The work once is why I am emailing you for all of the reason.)
'No Charge No Fix' in priority of my Ad on top is I could choose customer. Like this if alone myself could guarantee income to be covered living costs of family members even

selecting customers easily would be the most desirable. In fact, my refrigeration work has been done for 20 years immediately after immigration of here beginning in January 2002. I had Googl Ads Account opened on 31 March 2019, because my ad of Local Newspaper classified was reached uppermost limit, and had been started our relationship.

Beginning of 5 months my ad was always positioned on Top page in Search title as it was. Subsequently advisement expenses were increased to $1,150.00 by 2.3 times, but monthly Sales amount were about $10,000.00 which was nearly no difference in comparison with Local paper Ad peak season.

However, after around 5 months my Ad on Top page previously was frequently moved positioning on the back page 2 – 5. At that time I was wondering why Appliance company of free ad even $1.00 positioned in my initial location even though there was its Search title separately. I don't understand above happening took place even though "Refrigerator Repair Only" of my company which paying $1,150.00 monthly. Free of ad fee Appliance company deprives me of my position, moreover mine is pushed back 4-5 pages. Is it reasonable?

Occasionally I could find my 'Seoul Refrigeration' under company name 'Tauranga Appliance' where is located 140km apart from here.

I had promised I could do work service within 20km when I joined opening Ads Account. Sometimes I get a call-out request from Taupo where is apart 200km from here. Of course, I can not meet their request. I made a rule North and West out of service amongst Auckland regions. One day, budget was filled with number of clicks but there was no calling even wrong phone call. Same situation has often been occurred. In this case my Ad was pushed back to page 3-4 without exception. This is a peculiarity of my Ad concerned. You know those phenomena well because you are continuously monitoring them.

21 October 2019

There was a first video phone meeting with Abrah between 1:00pm – 3:30pm. In the meeting I raised my Ad positioning, and he told me "It will be time taken because I have to report this issue to Headquarter."

However, there was no change updated. So, I sent Claiming-mail to Ton & Abrah 6 times between December 2020 and April 2021, but I have never gotten their responses even just once.

05 May 2021

There was second video teleconference with Abrah between 5:20pm – 6:30pm. He promised that he could fix it on the first page while it's difficult put my ad positioning on the top of the first page as I raised the same.

However, the promise was broken within just 2 days. So, I sent mail to press him to fulfill the promise on 07 May, 10 May continuously. But he never responded me my email.

On 21 May 2021, I had my Ad suspended for 10 days notifying to keep the promise or Ad stop. But the promise never kept. From then I had been considering to stop Ad begging and closing my business. Because income would be zero if there were no ads in characteristics of business of mine.

28 July 2021

Through correspondence with Senior Account Strategist Shan Sams we decided to hold a video teleconference following day.

29 July 2021

In the first teleconference meeting with Shan setup Budget $45 from $33.3/day. Subsequently my Ad fee adjusted to $1,570.00/monthly from $1,150.00/m, and Max. CPC bid limitation to $4 from $2.33 sharply in his recommendation. I questioned about this adjustment but he told me I could get a merit for comparative bid with other rival companies.

And, as a result, a normal positioning had been lasted for 22 days till 20 August.

21 August 2021

Again it went back to previous worsened situation.

23 and 30 August

I sent mail to be kept the promise. And it seemed to be normal.

23 September 2021, around 1:00pm

On driving I got a call from Shan, he requested me to change my translator. I answered my translator was New Zealand JP(Justice of the Peace) currently, and trustworthy to community people, excellent translator. And I asked him to email me telling me the reason why changing translator.

Upon arrival home I read the E-mail he sent in which the reason was ridiculous and also the request was very dangerous I thought.

27 September 2021

I sent him a mail like this "I apologize about troublesome issues make it, I accept your request …"

The reason why I accepted his inappropriate request I expected my Ad was to be fixed normally if I accepted it in return for. But my request appealing was thoroughly ignored instead of reward.

Lastly I sent an email with just 3 words in a sentence 'Please help me' on 9 December, after 29/09, 18/10, 20/10, 25/10, 27/10, 28/10, 31/10, 05/11, 06/11, 23/11 and 30/11.

Now, beginning of off-season, I am going to decide stopping begging Googl Ads anymore, and close my business before April next year. I have never changed once my decision or revised it in my life so far. It is because I make a decision after fully reviewing & taking a consideration in every matter.

10 November 2021

This day is the day to encounter a worst woman whom I must not meet to. She is owner of a Gas Station under the name of Xue WU. If my Ad ran a classified properly, I might be worked repairing 2-3 refrigerators a day in November peak season. But I couldn't get worked chance even a fridge repair for 2 days. I would be refused her lie which work I evade when usual day going, but I was induced to come her place even with an appointment. However, she intentionally fled onsite after sending a photo of there while her puppet husband was turning up the same place. Thus ill-fated relationship with her began.

You could see if this incident is what relation with you after reviewing titled 'Last Mail' to Bharga which I sent it on 24 June 2022.

5 January 2022

I sent a mail to Shan with New Year's greetings. Once more I raised a reasonable suggestion based on statistics. And I proved how my currently financial crisis was being serious, too. Also, I explained why I have to keep continuing my business in detail.

However, he ignored even the reasonable suggestion.

I hope you read this mail which I sent it to Bharga again.

25 April 2022
I received a mail from Bharga in which was booked a telephone consultation. But I didn't reply on that mail because I was ongoing Disputes Tribunal process with 'Xue WU' mentioned before while I already decided to close my business effective on 31 March 2022.

24 June 2022
Please read one more time this mail to Bharga this day due to the same to previous mail.

28 June 2022, Noon
Refer to Mail I sent to Vinee

28 June 2022, 5:45pm
Refer to Mail I sent to Bharga

5 August 2022
I requested Business Profile Team to delete 4 negative comments I was not interested in because I have to close my business immediately after judgement in Court. I had to respond positively the trial because there was a Xue WU's deliberate negative comment among those previously mentioned.

5 September 2022
Refer to Mail I sent to Bharga

12 September 2022
Refer to E-mail I sent to Bharga

Hello, Sharu !
You maybe look down upon my Ad fee $1,570.00 a month, but it is over 25% of my Monthly Sales total amount. In my business characteristics there is not only big difference of income according to Ad positioning but also my income would be zero if there's no advertisement. You may know my income how much seeing the Business Pro. Team's monthly Report. You must know customers linked to actual income could be less than a half. You may also imagine it well as I previously explained.

I don't know what do you think of $1million which is a house value, but it is valuable money to be divided to a thousand people by $1,000. We must know the fact a thousand dollar is higher valuable to needed poor person than a million dollar of a rich man.

'I put aside even the humble dream.'

All of relationships are beginning and the end.
Being uncomfortable in any process should not be left as regretful to the end.

I want to say goodbye Bharga with happiness.

Kind regards

Young Soo Youn / Seoul Refrigeration

 youngsoo youn <seoulref@gmail.com>

The Last Mail
1개의 메일

youngsoo youn <seoulref@gmail.com>   2022년 6월 24일 오후 1:01
받는사람: Bharga Kokkiligad <kokkiligad @googl .com>

Dear Bharga,
I welcome your reaching my Ads account as new representative.
My ID is 454-387-6821 Seoul Refrigeration, Youngsoo Youn. I have continuously raised an issue of my ads position while it was being advertised on Googl Ads for last 3 years and a month. My last appeal it to be solved out was that I sent an E-mail titled as 'Suggestion' to Shan on 5th January this year, and I haven't been doing appeal to Googl anymore.
In the mean time I had been phone-call meeting with Abrah twice and Shan once. The promises on that meetings didn't kept in fact, and moreover they never responded on my numerous complain mails.
I can't maintain my business without advertising on Googl Ads, and if the promises were broken my business income is to be decreased on pressure of finance in my business characteristics as a result.
Please understand this reason of the point is not the main reason that I must close my business. However, I am recovering peace of mind because I was diminished my lifestyle to humble after giving up good deeds for others in difficulty, as mentioned in the end of the suggestion on last 5th January, through my business work in my life lastly. Making a decision to be part of the ranges I have to pay back bank mortgage & private loan recently occurred after selling my property which I live in, instead giving up my plan to do good things for other persons in difficulties. I am sure the rest of money could be making me enjoying my rest of life exercise for health such as playing golf after buying a small house nearby golf course.
My business could be closed after coming out of the judgement, as of now, as I am under the process of a trial situation involved in recent surroundings of mine unexpectedly. This lawsuit is very badly unusual person involved who requested a small job on me even though peak season these days. Dispute of the job between the customer and me made me directly to file a suit against her in Court.
2nd Hearing will be falling on 8th July next month, my aim over the hearing is returning for as much as unfortunate of mine I must close my business. Because, doing so only, I can move forward to rest of my life. By the way there is one thing I am concerning which is Additional Evidence submitted to Court in. In there "My advertising media" is involved in this part. Of course, this part was nothing to do with the issue which was wrote during explanation of my routine business work activities.
However, all of documents submitted in court were immediately sharing with other party according to the rule. Therefore I think she and her legal aid are getting extreme out of control to dash her defense in all means. Except those things there would be also ill-advised later, so I am informing you of this issue through mail in advance.
I am keep G-mail sent correspondence with involved persons so far in mail box. Ton and Abraha Gaj 's mails between 03/12/2020 – 21/05/2021, and also Shan Sams 's mail between 28/07/2021 – 05/01/2022 are in the mail box. And, all of those mails will be deleted immediately.
I am planning to expose her disappeared conscience through SNS after closing my business. The reason why other competitive companies throw unpleasant look at me because my position in Statistics Summary Impression Share is on Top. Meanwhile I was already ostracized like in the service market caused by her range of bad behavior. In fact, I have been facing explicit Cold reception from suppliers for nearly 6 months after the matters exposed.
Those facts are the reasons I must close my business and she must be committed twiticide.
First of all I will be posting SNS the sentencing. Secondly certificate & graph recorded my ability in comparison. And, thirdly, her mocking me my qualification & ability as mentioned above. I will be showing those before 2-3 days of SNS posting. That means it is just for your information if any.
At the time, I will be appreciated you if you help me requesting in details with Free Ads, my address, phone number, my GPS location information and delete function… etc.
I will not be emailing you until then anymore.
For your information, let me attach the mail sent Shan as 'Suggestion' titled.
Kind regards

Young Soo Youn

📎 **suggestion (05 01 2022).pdf**
68K

보낸 사람: 윤 영수
보낸 날짜: 2022년 1월 5일 수요일 오후 1:11
받는 사람: shan point
제목: Suggestion

Dear Shan

Happy New Year!

I wish you good things with you of this New Year after difficulties of the Covid-19 last year.
As I settle account all of last 2 years and 8 months' Googl Ads, I cordially request your help while I suggest 2 issues as follows which is better improved results for afterwards.

The reason why I must advertise as Title "Fridge Freezer Repair Only" through Googl Ads is the only way I could let customers know me whom they needed my unique service only I can do.

I had made my Will testament in which I filled my hope of completing of my Final Task in life about the time after 6 months since opening Googl Ads Account from 31 March 2019. Because the background was that my Ad was always located at the top fixed of the page in "Fridge Freezer Repair" of Googl Search Section title, First page of Cell Phone and the top of the second page of Computer Screen.

The reason why I think this positioning is extremely natural that all other business companies have their own special advertisement space while I also take part in Googl Ads.

However, 2 years' going by 2nd year I had frequently seen only my ad was gradually pushed back as unstable positioning. Consequently, I could maintain the status quo followingly about -15% monthly total sales in comparison with monthly period of the previous year.

And from last April entering 3rd year, 5 parts of my Ad search such as 'Fridge Freezer Repair Auckland', '— Central Auck.', '— East Auck.', '— South Auck.' & 'Commercial Fridge

Freezer Repair Auckland' were not the same previously that is to say position changing by rotation frequently. In other words all searched cases like previously were rare, and part by part rotated onto other pages except first or second page even 8th page, and sometimes skipping showed irregular positioning.

At last my Ad nearly couldn't find at all parts of section on Computer Screen from last October.

The result recorded about minus 30% monthly total sales in comparison with the same month of First year. This made me to face financial difficulties seriously.

This unusual situation is my first experience of undergoing through my one-way career of 45 years continuously.

Eventually I've got an urgent loan from my main bank to cover $1,000 of Googl Ads advertisement fee which is direct debited withdrawal from my account on every 18th of the month. (*a Photo attached)

However, this is just a stopgap measure which is not a fundamental way becoming.

Therefore, my first suggestion is requesting that my Ad should be returned to normal positioning like as first 8 months period of 2019.

AD Contents, Service method and so on were not different from the beginning until now.

Change things were that Budget was changed to $45/day from $33.30/day, and Max. CPC Bid Limit from $2.33 to $4.

My second suggestion is that I request to except me at Bid Statistics Daily Report. The reasons; Firstly I have no qualification to take a part in the steps because I am running one person company for a living while other companies are organized for making a profit gain. How can I compete with them or being in comparison with different purpose & condition?

Second reason is that my business work statistics have many variables in characteristics of my Ad because even if there are many clicks of hit they are not match for working in reality out of imagination a few results faraway my expectation.

Then let us have a look below October & November 2021 Performance Report sent by Googl Business Profile Team as follows;

2021	Interaction	Real customer in my diary
October	74 persons	23 persons
November	100 persons	21 persons

Diary Record 2019		Real customer
October	05/10 ~ 31/10	26 persons
November	01/11 ~ 30/11	32 persons

According to above chart, Relations between Interaction and Real customer are non-proportion.

Definitely I find the relation between First page coverage and Real customer is very close.

As seeing above chart, because one of my specific statistics is giving a negative influence to Reliability of Statistics needs Accuracy, I am requesting your authority to except me.

I personally so appreciate Googl 's giving me a Benefit for my business. The reason why I was destined to leave my family while everybody in his or her twilight years out of working. Then Googl gave me an opportunity to get vitality of my living and making me hope & feeling worthwhile to help neighbour's hardship.

My last task hereafter in 7 years is to distribute this my residing property to people needed help perfectly.

If all matters were normalized sooner or later I will be notarizing my Will in relation with 4 charities organizations made already 2 years ago. Because nobody knows old man's fate tomorrow. In there a record of Googl s support will also be left.

*1 attachment

 youngsoo youn <seoulref@gmail.com>

Request for Transferring to Bharga
2개의 메일

youngsoo youn <seoulref@gmail.com>   2022년 6월 28일 오후 12:07
받는사람: vvineet @google.com

Dear Vinee ,

My ID: 454-387-6421, Seoul Refrigeration Nm: Youngsoo Youn

I notified Bharga my situation and future plan which were required very important confidence 4 days ago (24th June).

This had done for predecessors Abraha and Shan , and furthermore for your company.

Because the negative contents of 'Ads media' which must be left in Court records were inclusive if the other and I share them. In case, if we eliminate key point concerned of the E-mail there is no problem.

Essential point is that if the E-mail contents sent Bharga . 4 days ago were regarded seen first time the problem could be solved out simply after treating Shan· didn't check it.

I already completed measures of mine I must take.

And 2 requests described in the E-mail should be carried out. If it would be difficult even fixing position only on cell phone & computer is reasonable to me.

My ultimatum will be taken within a month, at least two months.

I never want duty-staff changing until then because I promised Bharga

If there will be messing with the plan, I am notifying, I can not cover protection of yours.

   ● Please convey my corrective measure attached to Bharga   *

Kind regards

Young Soo Youn

첨부파일 14 개

after_1.jpg
3694K

before_1.jpg
3353K

 Gmail   youngsoo youn <seoulref@gmail.com>

Seoul Refrigeration - Youngsoo Youn
2개의 메일

Bharga Kokkiligad.. <kokkiligad @googl com>   2022년 6월 28일 오후 3:12
받는사람: seoulref@gmail.com

Hi Youngsoo,

Thank you for your time over the phone today,

In reference to the call we had, I understand that you do not prefer a call from our end to discuss your concern, however I have limited access over email support.

The previous email "The Last Mail" was received but I would like to have a better understanding on what support is expected by you from our end so that i would be able to check with my Internal teams for the same.

If possible and if it is convenient for you, we can have a quick call scheduled and go through the same. Otherwise, Please let me know what is your concern and what support you require from our end regarding Googl Ads Account.

Awaiting your response.

schedule a

Regards,
Bharga

Work from Home & Stay Safe!!
Bharga   K | Account Strategist | Regalix supporting Googl | Third-Party Partners | kokkilig   ?googl ^om
| AU +6129160'   . | NZ +649870

---

youngsoo youn <seoulref@gmail.com>   2022년 6월 28일 오후 5:46
받는사람: Bharga   .<kokkiligad   @googl .com>

Dear Bharga ,

I don't like to talk about that previous broken promises or no(never) responses of your predecessors.

I was furious of no-response from Sha   regarding my "Suggestion" mail which was inclusive all of my requests on 5 January 2022. Also I was in a rage seriously that was becoming of direct cause of closing my business.

You may take a relevant action on my requests which were specified in the mail on 5th of January 2022 as it is.

If not possible, please let me know the reason why.

yoongsoo youn <seoulref@gmail.com>

review
1 개의 메일

yoongsoo youn <seoulref@gmail.com> 2022년 9월 5일 오후 5:05
받는사람: seoulref@hotmail.com

Dear Duty Staff on Google Business Profile Review,

Greetings

I am Young Soo Youn, Seoul Refrigeration.

There is a content of 'No Charge No Fix' in my Ads. This part is convenience that customer can get work schedule & a quotation through direct phone conversation between User and Technician. On the other hand, it should be all the time taken precaution there is a fact that always exposed to User who abuses it. Usually most of them are filtered at first phone conversation, and in case of realizing the intent onsite I could give up the job itself ended simply. However, there is rarely case that customer would not pay charge to find fault with misunderstanding technically after completion of repair.

Such a customer threatens constantly to post bad comment on my company involved inticing worker deliberately. I have the case closed, giving up repair cost not to deal with him or her as well as not scared of the customer.

Let me show reviewing of bad comments posted for 5 months recently as follows;

16 March 2022: M"Mez"   This person promised to pay repair cost $280.00 by online banking in the evening same day, but two days later he texted me the machine seemed to be abnormal. Immediately I realized the intent of the customer, and gave up the repair cost $280.00. And, 3 days later he posted Bad Tweet on Review to find fault with my business wackily.   *Refer to my response

11 May 2022: Trac Cui   This woman is a friend of Xuey Wu who counterclaimed over 3 times of the balance to Court. Xuey Wu made false documents to welch the balance $4,360.00 of my work. I had submitted this Bad Tweet to the court as an evidence.   *Refer to my response

7 August 2022: Ashleig Compagri   *Refer to my response

9 August 2022: Ala Young   *Refer to my response

Thus, I respectfully request Google to delete above 4 Bad Tweets and restore to my original credit rating, as you can, after referring to my representative response of my company.

 youngsoo youn <seoulref@gmail.com>

Asking for Handling Request of Review
2개의 메일

youngsoo youn <seoulref@gmail.com>   2022년 9월 5일 오후 5:15
받는사람: Bharga Kokkilig <kokkiligad @googl .com>

Dear Bharga

How are you these days?

I sent followings to Googl Business Profile Team by G-mail on 12 August 2022.

(Photo 1) (Photo 2) (gmail 1) (gmail 2)

However, I didn't receive any response from them until today, 5 September 2022, passed not 3 business days but 24 days.

I had informed you my situation & plan in detail through G-mail on 24 June 2022 and 28 June 2022. Messages twice through the G-mail I want to let you know were the points that uncomfortable relationship between Googl Ads and me for last 3 years would be winding up clearly while my business was under the closing.

But I am so disappointing and express my regret at you Googl 's attitude in absolute ignoring the humble request of mine till today.

Kind regards

Young Soo Youn

첨부파일 4 개

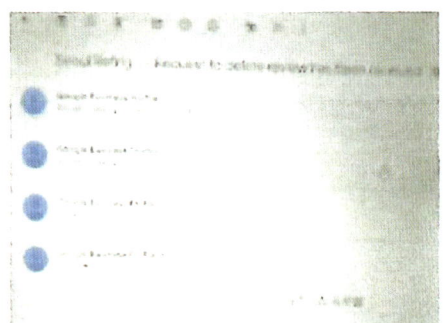

Photo 1.jpg
359K

Photo 2.jpg
378K

gmail 1.jpg
119K

gmail 2.jpg
15K

---

youngsoo youn <seoulref@gmail.com>
받는사람: Bharga Kokkiligad <kokkiligad @googl .com>

2022년 9월 12일 오전 11:25

Subj.: Reminder E-mail

Greetings

I emailed you on 5 September 2022 lastly.

However, any action haven't taken since then and also I didn't receive any response from you so far.

As of now Court judgement is just around corner, and please do me a favor of my last request for deleting 4 deliberately negative comments against me.

So, my credit rating could normally be recovered as you take an action.

Looking forward to hearing from you.

Kind regards

Young Soo Youn

[받은메일 숨김]

첨부파일 4 개

A deletion request is being processed

Photo 1.jpg
359K

Handling account assistance
3개의 메일

Sharukh. Kha <sharukhkh.@googl..com> 2022년 9월 13
받는사람: seoulref@gmail.com

Hi,

This is Sharu. kha , your Account Strategist here at Googl Ads. I tried calling you a couple of times but thought that email might be the best reach you.

Please reply to this email with a date and time to schedule a call so that we can deep dive into the account and work on amplifying the perform

Looking forward to hearing from you.

-Thank you,

Sharukh Kh. . | Senior Account Strategist | Regalix supporting Googl. | GCS-Googl Ads (UMM-APAC)
Third-Party Partners
Australia : +6127250
Newzealand: +6448062
Email sharukhkh. @googl. om

---

youngsoo youn <seoulref@gmail.com> 2022년 9월
받는사람: Sharuk Kha. <sharukhkh. @googl com>

Dear Sharu ,

Thank you for your email & suggestion of date and time to schedule for my account strategy. However, the best way for that would be email correspondence because English is my second language. As I experienced calling basis before the conversation and understanding were very limited.

Hence, please email me regarding this and any other anytime and so, I will be replying immediately as I could do.

Looking forward to hearing from you.
Very kind regards

Young Soo Youn / Seoul Refrigeration

Sharuk. Kh. <sharukhkh. @googl .com> 2022년 9월 19일 오후 12:48
받는사람: youngsoo youn <seoulref@gmail.com>

Hello Youngsoo,

I completely understand that it is difficult for you to have a conversation in English, however I urge you to please provide your available time so that we can discuss more about the issue.

As to raise any request from our end we need to isolate the issue and raise it to the concerned department.

Awaiting your response.

[받은메일 숨김]
--
[받은메일 숨김]

The Fact & Email

1. I, applicant Youngsoo Youn, emailed 'The Fact' titled to 5 Major Suppliers in which contained evidence proving documents and newly added the last Evidence that were proved respondent Xue Wu's wrongful acts as I already submitted them to Court for a last year.   (Attachment 1)

   Purpose of mailing was to dispel speculation and misunderstanding they got through rumor issues in relation to Wu around. To give advance notice a day before, I visited 5 companies, and met 3 managers of each company and got 'Okay' from them all. I didn't see the other 2 managers due to their absence during my visiting their companies.

   However, Manager of 'R' company who mostly welcomed in expecting changed his mind in a day. So I didn't convey my email message to him because of mail message rejection on. Immediately after, I emailed the other 2 companies which were in manager absences my request to 'ignore' the Email.   (Attachment 2)

   The reason why sending additional email for ignorance I became aware of embarrassments of the supply companies later because there were contained their trading company 'P' Refrigeration and 'W' Refrigeration in relation with their irrelevant acts in the Email
   (The two companies that accepted my email believed that there would be no business with 'W' or 'P' refrigeration because their supply sources were different or their prices were relatively high.)

2. Suppliers are being secondary to Technicians on-site with technical knowledge. In other words, they are qualified persons who could professionally make a judgement for the issue of like Wu's issue this time objectively. And they all know me well because they were introduced me as a customer from their seniors.

   Owing to this Email sending, relating with Wu & me, and other persons as well and furthermore all of refrigeration businesses became aware of Wu's bad acts in detail.

3. My decision of Email sending to Suppliers was that because Wu ridiculed my qualification and capability at insult deliberately with wrongful technical information she made.   I indicated those in my Evidence documents I already submitted to Court.

4. I thought this work was better than nothing even though this was not related to

the trial result after long waiting for it through hearings referee instructed me to wait for the result within 4 weeks, and a month waiting at Last Hearing. Finally I sent it on 2nd February 2023, 2 month later The hearing.

Postscript

(This postscript was written along with 8. Petition of Appeal.)

1. I, applicant Youngsoo Youn, see I had clearly proved respondent Xue Wu's deliberately lasted fraudulent practices through 'Last Evidence & Images Collection'. Thus confirming way of Wu's falsehood and deceiving behavior became very simple. Even though any normal investigator who absolutely does not have technique could give proof of Wu's fraudulent practices through 3 ways of on-site confirmation only.

Wu told, "I must use the Freezer because it is peak season." at Last Hearing.

1) Did inspector spot inspection in surprise visit the onsite if it was currently on operation? If it had not been used or there was no plan to use it after repairment (eg. got a quotation for it?) Wu has this incident upsized so far by thinking initially not use it as well as telling a lie in the Hearing.

2) If she is currently using it after repairing which part of it? If the Controller repaired or replaced of it by new one she deceived Referee in collusion with Whit · Refrigeration. Moreover it would be proved that she has continuously been committed a fraud to bilk the balance even following my instruction in my Report with her fake Report, exaggerated Quote, altered reports..etc for last a year.

3) Anybody could confirm Cover of Condensing Unit on the issue of rooftop. If there is the Cover it would be proved she has continuously been committed a fraud with lie from the beginning up to now for one year and 2 months.

2. All matters so far are extremely common sense, absolutely not technical matter. As far as all evidences of incident are on the spot there is a possibility to confirm them anytime in as previously mentioned. To put it another way, when wrong decision revealed later then Referee will should be put up with fatal responsibility.

This is also the reason why I lodge an appeal.

3. I, applicant Youngsoo Youn, demand to punish following persons or company based on the Evidence I submitted if their offence done.

*Xue Wu   *Anan Choha   *Pete Refrigeration

*Whit Refrigeration   *Trac Cui

4. I, applicant Youngsoo Youn, plead to get a chance for reapplying with this modified appellant appeal exchange it I already submitted. If I were allowed to reapply after getting Order of extension of Court filing I will immediately be reapplying a new written Appeal briefly within 2 days. Then exchanged corresponding part of old one would be scrapped and completely deleted from mine & translator's PDF file. Corresponding part here means the part related to Referee mentioned on front part of it in which "I thought distribution of time was unfair in 1st & 2nd Hearings." described. Except that part there will absolutely not be mentioned about Referee.

(4. above was deleted when the second appeal was filed.)

5. I, applicant Youngsoo Youn, directly submitted a PITITION to Court on 18th October 2022. In there I proved Evidence in detail attaching mail correspondence with Googl team, that was to say "The fact that Googl Ads team continuously harassed advertiser with irrelevant unfair way in systematically."

Please review detailed breakdown of this story again, and I would like to convey a strong warning message to the Googl Ads team from the Court in which they could be under inditement because of their deed which were numerously ignoring my complaints for around last 3 years, tyranny of pressure on change of my essential personnel, and to be closing situation of my business due to deterioration of profitability caused by their breaking promise if they were against the law. Nevertheless, there is no reason or intention I raise getting into trouble legally.

I have no more desire if all of this work were to be a greeting for farewell as level of Justice disclosing for me one way life of 45 years' Refrigeration career lastly.

보낸 사람: 윤 영수
보낸 날짜: 2023년 2월 2일 목요일 오후 4:04
받는 사람: Lorraine Sifou; ekumer@realcold.co.nz; Craig.Parker@reece.co.nz; arnz@pattonnz.com; Mike Hines
제목: The Fact

(ATT.1)

Dear Sir / Madam

First of all, I endlessly appreciate you that I have continuously been running my business very good owing to your support & cheering for last 20 years.

Especially we all are aware of the reality that we overcome hardships due to Covid Pandemic these days. Meanwhile I have been suffering double torture even now for last a year more or less after being involved in a really absurd matter is still awaited.

Therefore I would like to share the truth of this event through 'The Fact' with all of you

Kind regards

Youngsoo Youn

보낸 사람: 윤 영수
보낸 날짜: 2023년 2월 3일 금요일 오전 8:15
받는 사람: Mike Hines
제목: Ignore the email

(ATT.2)

Good morning, Mike

I am sorry for the interruption. Please ignore my previous email. Thank you

iOS용 Outlook 다운로드

Petition of Appeal

Case number: CIV-2021-055-000

Applicant   Youngsoo Youn

Seoul Refrigeration

Respondent   Xue Wu

C/ - BP Meadowban Station

Reason of Appeal

I, applicant Youngsoo Youn, was treated very unfairly from Referee through 1st & 2nd Hearing. The referee, moreover, completely ignored my material & realistic evidences which I applicant had submitted four times for last a year. She also accepted respondent Xueyi Wu's false manipulative evidence 100% which was submitted by herself. Therefore, I lodge an appeal with an additional evidence attached against result of the judgement.

(The above is the deleted part of the second appeal submitted to the court.)

1. I called up Wu's couple 2 days before finishing the installation work on purpose, and promised Bank Transfer immediately after reaching -20°C.

2. Wu broke the promise made 2 days ago, furthermore she made a fake issue colluded with an unqualified person in wrongful technical information, and she had Equipment which was installed all demolished. And she threatened me to refund $4,000.00 which she paid in the middle.

3. Then I told her the fact I filed Court against her 6 days before. She, this time, submitted a false manipulative document in which amount showing over 3 times of the balance to Court as a Counter Claim.

4. 16th February 2022 < 1st Hearing >

    Referee listened Wu's story which is far from essence unlimitedly except 'destruction of fulfillment of Contract' which is essential part of the issue

(She was helping Wu's story indefinitely, probably without any sanctions, and during my turn to speak, she pressured me by saying, "There is no time, so just finish it briefly!")

Then the hearing closed 15 minutes earlier than schedule while about 20 minutes left to the end. I guess Wu's speaking time was at least over 3 times than me.

(The parenthesis above is the deleted part of the second appeal submitted to the court.)

5. 11th Aprill 2022

   In a letter I sent Referee I technically explained in detail that a controversial issue of 'Wrong Condensing Unit' Wu insisted was absolutely wrong. And in the letter I indirectly expressed my feeling that there was unjust in 1st Hearing.

6. Wu and her accomplice Anan got to know their written false controversial issue was wrong, and this time submitted a fake manipulative report to Court approaching Whit Refrigeration.

7. 2nd December 2022 < 2nd Hearing >

   2nd Hearing, after 1 year and a day since my filing court, was absolutely the same as 1st Hearing. In other words it had been proceeded being averted its nature fact.

8. I could presume somewhat the result of this trial through the last Hearing. Therefore I determined to prepare for Petition of Appeal destined in gathering Wu's last evidence of evil deed from the beginning to end.

9. Order of Disputes Tribunal found in my letterbox on 8th February 2023 was result content which it was far beyond my common sense.

(10. The 'rebuttal' to the 'details of payment order' written in the first appeal submitted to the court has been deleted.)

***(The date the referee issued 'the Order' was 02/12/2022.
This was the day the last hearing was held and it was also
the day she declared that
"I would make a decision and notify me within 4 weeks."
I received 'the Order' two months and six days later.
The date 'the Order' was received was also
46 days past the deadline for appeal.)***

Last Evidence (case number: CIV-2021-055-000   )

Applicant: Youn, Youngsoo

   Seoul Refrigeration owner

Respondent: Wu, Xue

   BP Meadowban Gas Station owner

< Event Outline >

1. Respondent Xue Wu's Freezer Room Equipment which was a Party Ice Pack Storage (exclusive use) Equip. being out of date and abolition of use from all fuel/gas stations long time ago. Instead, excellent Chest Freezer which is located at entrance outside of all of stations, Ice factory hires and manages free of charge it to them. You may easily see it at any fuel stations in NZ. Especially System Equip like Wu's Freezer Room Equip doesn't need, and it must not to be used even it was completed. It is absolutely unnecessary equipment these days. For example, Ice Storage volume of big supermarket PAK'nSAVE or Countdown is much smaller size than Wu's by 1/20 occupying space, moreover it could physically be seen as quite different structure of fan invisible which is decreasing airflow extremely.
(1-1) (1-2) (1-3)

2. As above seen respondent Xue Wu, even though she knew the fact that it's unnecessary Equip. probably got bad and selfish thought which could be completed fixing her much troubled Freezer Room equipment with only one unit replacing amount to pay attention of noticeable Ad phrase 'No charge No fix' though searching Googl Ads of mine myself Youngsoo Youn, while she was suffered long-term cessation from several breakdowns of units of her own Freezer Room equipment.

She approached me in advance preparation deliberately, and she went away after luring me with lie avoiding direct confrontation. And the Install work was started with only one unit replacing while she didn't pay even $1.00 in her successful intelligent methodology.

(2-1) (2-2) (2-3) (2-4)

3. I had been pushed around by Wu's trap with an Install work which could be completed in just 6 hours but staggering in 17 days by her terrible money play continuously.

4. Wu, 2 days before completion of Install work, showed plain brazen she easily broke in just 2 days even a reasonable promise that she should immediately pay off balance $4,360.00 instead of Free Replace of $3,000.00 worth Unit as my way to free myself accuser from her Evil hand.

(4-1) (4-2)

5. I, applicant, sent an E-mail enclosed 'Official Operating Report' & 'Urging fulfillment of promise' to respondent Wu to be reviewed in advance, and I directly visited her appealing to her conscience lastly. But she cracked a little smile in relaxed facial expression on the day differently from previous attitude that she didn't eye contact nor greetings passing by for 17 days previously as if 'I am in no hurry now for it anymore because I confirmed reaching promised -20°C'.

6. Respondent Xueyi Wu began to reveal her actual character at last. She sent me a terrible chantage E-mail in the middle of the night.

(6-1) (6-2)

7. I, applicant, told her 'Without paying off the balance You must not use the equipment of touch' in following day. And noticed her by email the fact that I filed a complaint against her to Dispute Tribunal Court.

(7-1) (7-2)

8. Wu did below 1), 2), and 3) a month away 1st Hearing;

    1) A fake Inspection Report which wrote by unqualified person

    2) Wholly wrong fake Report that the Condensing Unit wrote by unqualified person was chosen wrongfully.

3) Manipulated Quote sheet wrote by 'P. Refrigeration' inflated 2 steps

Wu submitted counter claim documents based on above three with $13,339.00 over 3 times of $4,360.00 which she was responsible to pay it to me.
(8-1) (8-2) (8-3) (8-4)

9. Anan of Chill36 Ltd who wrote a fake Report is certainly a worker of HVAC, not Refrigeration as he does not hold the Electrical Service Technician License. Because he conducted following action in which his license should be cancelled immediately if he were a license-holder relevantly. He planned and carried out irresponsible & bad conduct with Wu from the beginning, and at lastly Hearing, even after more than about a year, he masterminded Wu into the deadly situation to the end while he wouldn't showing the slightest bit of remorse anymore.

10. Wu wasted Hearing time over 3 times than me with different stories far from the key point which core issue of 'nonfulfillment of her promise' was excepted.

    (Refer to 1st Hearing recording file)

11. Wu, a month before 2nd Hearing scheduled, submitted correspondence E-mail amongst the unqualified person & Supplier Sales person and herself a day before that day in which she challenged to the statistics already submitted in 1st Evidence docs to prove my Certificate and Best Service technician objectively with the wholly faked Report, sneering my qualification and the ability in view of the wrong source of technical intelligence.
    (11-1)

12. Wu had strongly insisted that Select Condensing Unit was wholly wrong which was the biggest issue until then. But Wu had been recognized the fact of her insisting was wrong through by me myself -> Sales person -> previously unqualified person. Then this time after recognizing it as she approached W. Refrigeration and again attacked me with getting a description of the point of Controller breakdown in my report as 'there is no problem' of the company as well as wholly manipulating in the Report.
    I, applicant, specified a parts of the Controller issue in my Report.
    This is absurd, since Wu and the unqualified Anan know very well as to the

Controller issue. She intended seemingly to bilk money balance $4,360.00 immediately after she made aware of the controller problem solving through my Report. (Refer to Clause 10 of 2nd Additional Evidences)
(12-1) (12- 2)

13. Wu made an IP holder assumed one of her friends post bad comments against me on Googl Business Review to prepare another attacking issue in later 2nd Hearing, dropping my credit rating. Googl Profile Team promised for my deletion request positively taking about 3 days, but I got an answer in 32 days from the team there was no reason it would be deleted. So it has still been posted as it was.
(13-1)

14. Last 2nd Hearing on 02/12/22, Wu again misled essential story, wasting much time while she was revealing all of her insists not to pay the balance were lies by herself testifying decisively as a result.
The testimony showed Wu said "Due date for the balance payment was on 29/11/22 in the statement" mentioning 15/11/22 statement which was previously written before the promise. However, the immediate payment day of the balance was 23/11/21 actually. (Refer to 2nd Hearing recording file)
(14-1)

15. As another story of Googl. Business Team them hard to understand their handling work, Googl Ads team's systematical frequent failures to keep their promise and tyranny ignoring a lot of complaints of mine. The team led to meet Xue Wu destined.
(The story related to that in detail was wrote in the attached Petition.)

16. Lastly I myself, as a Service person for last 20 years here in NZ, have been abided by related regulations, and I would like to make public the Certificate of mine and Statistics of Googl. Ads graph & chart to which prove that I've gotten support & love from numerous customers of Central, East and South Auckland.
(16-1) (16-2) (16-3)

Like above Xue Wu has financially been inflicted on me and stained an innocent worker's honor of me seriously for her benefit with all means & ways in conspiracy with Unqualified person, No license. Also she had unreasonably been requesting related company and individual causing breached the rule for last one year.

Hence I am raising an application against her as I extremely hope Court dish out punishment severely on her Wu not to do such a bad things again anymore.

Next Pages are the evidence images collection;

Applicant   Youn, Young Soo

(The last evidence above was prepared before receipt of the Order.)

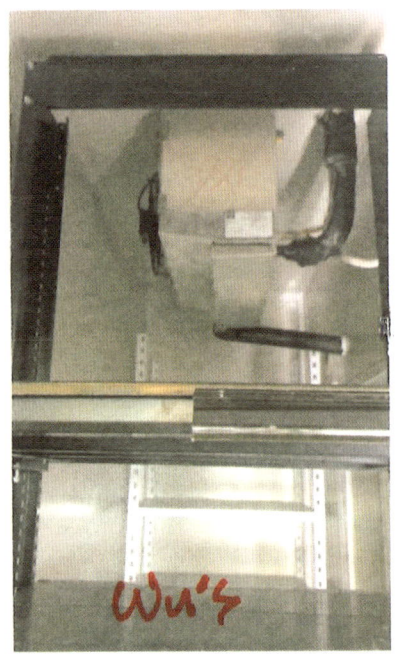
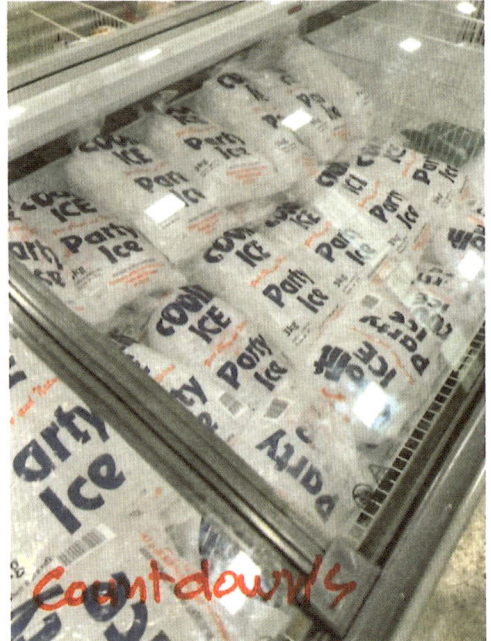
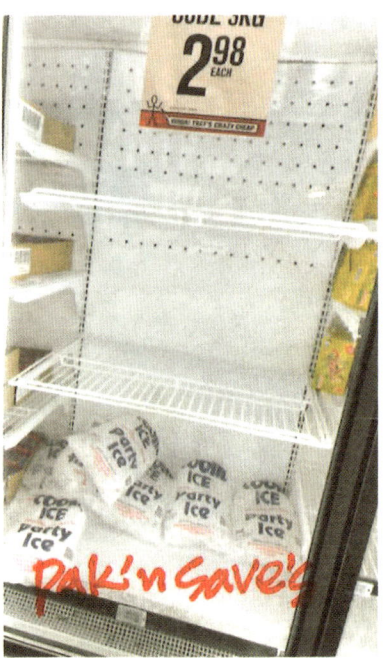

1-1   1-2   1-3

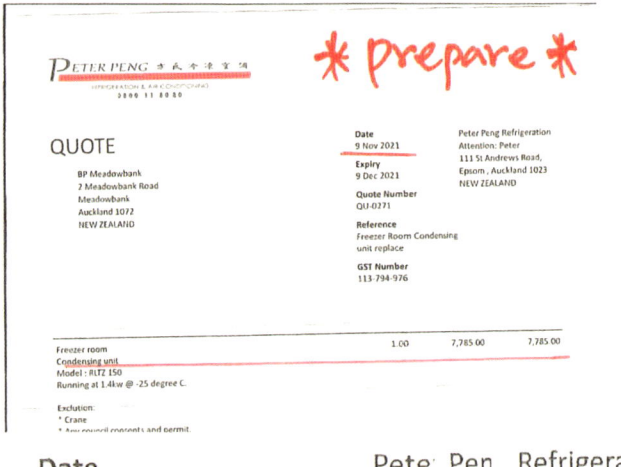

2-1   2-2

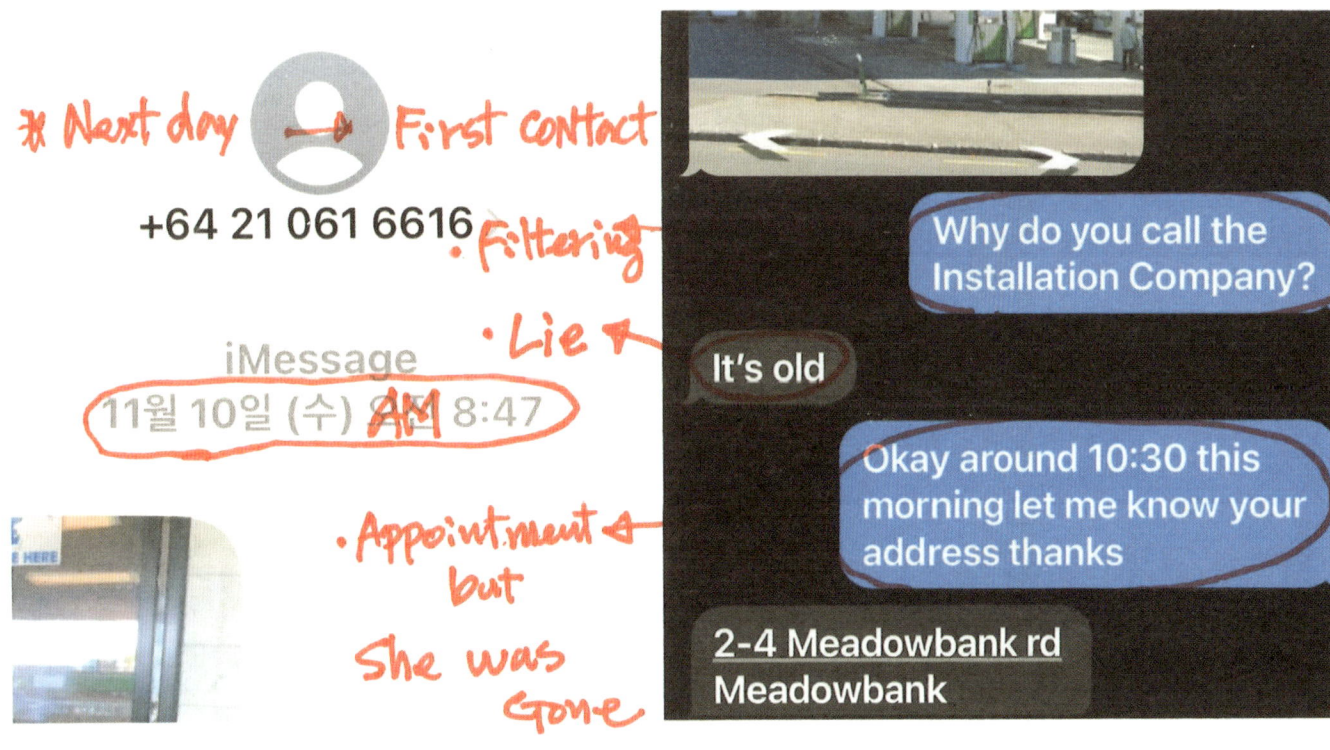

2-3   2-4

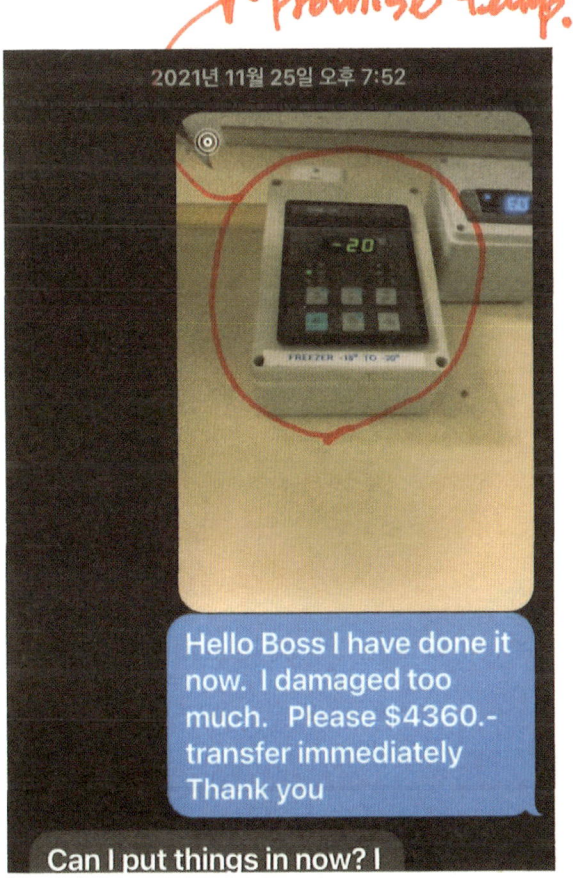

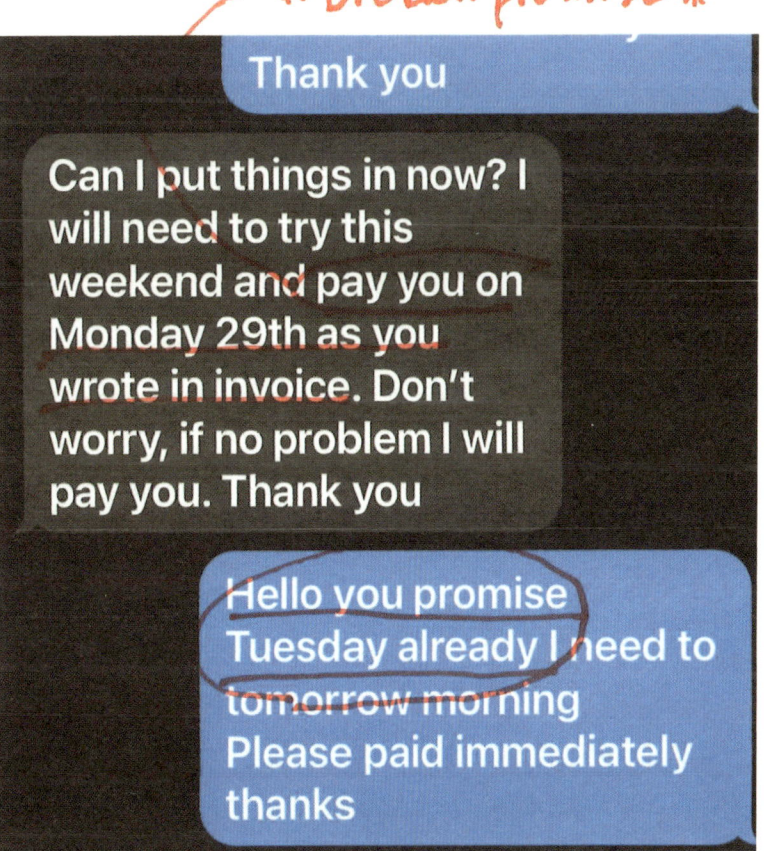

4-1   4-2

Fake Report

CHILL 36 LTD

PO BOX. HIGHBROOK, AUCKLAND. NZ
Ph 09 262. Fax 09 271 Cell 0216.
E Mail : ana @frigie.com # Web : www.frigie.com

INSPECTION REPORT

TO WHOMESOEVER IT MAY CONCERN

To,
BP Meadowbank,
2 Meadowbank road,
Remuera,
Auckland.

Date of Inspection : 04 December 2021

Upon my inspection on site regarding the new installation, I found following points.

1. The outdoor compressor Condensing unit is not suitable for the Freezer Application.
2. Condenser size is for Medium temp application not low temp,
3. No fan speed controller,
4. No oil separator.
5. No suction accumulator
6. Wrong compressor for Freezer application.
7. The suction Pipe insulation is also for the medium temp application.
8. The Expansion Valve sensor is not connected with company recommended and supplied clamp to tighten with the pipe.
9. No P trap for the suction pipe after the evaporator for compressor oil return
10. Evaporator front supply is too close to the opposite wall, which restricts the air flow to the product area and short cycle supply & return air.
11. The penetration hole is wrapped with duct tape which may get distorted in future by heat and UV rays and cause leak in the building. It needs to be installed by goose neck or roof hat kit.
12. Expansion valve super heat is not adjusted,
13. The tag of orifice no. is not attached to the expansion valve.
14. Mounting of Evaporator unit os to close to the front wall.

Summary :
The use of the main components & materials are completely noncompatible for the application of Freezer and the installation is unprofessional.

No Licence Number

For,
CHILL36 LTD

Xue Wu
받는 사람 나

2021년 12월 7일

7/12/2021

Threatening Mail

Dear Youngsoo (Seoul Refrigeration)

I had a professional from another refrigeration company do the inspections on Saturday 4/12/2021. He found the problem is the condensing unit. You bought incorrect condensing unit which is designed for medium temperature, not for low temperature.

Therefore, my requests are as below:

1. Take your condensing unit and inside cooler unit away.

2. Immediately refund my payment $4000 when you take away your units.

3. Reimbursement costs for inspections and report.

My business need to run. If you do not fulfill my requests by 5pm Sunday 12/12/2021, I will ask third party to remove your units and install new units. Neither third party nor I will take responsibility if the machines are damaged.

Regards
Xue

Response

윤 영수 <seoulref@hotmail.com> 于2021年12月8日 周三下午10:14写道：

I had completed the work in my responsibility complying with contents of our contract as dropping to -20 degree C promised temperature on 25th November 2021, 7:48pm, after finishing work all in duty.

And I emailed 'Report of Freezing System Operation, in which problem solution method in detail. On same day I explained letting you know face to face the problem in detail, visiting directly your workplace.

However, you refused to pay the balance $4360.00 while did not do anything to solve the problem on your duty at all to keep doing wrongful behavior intending not to pay it afterwards, either.

The Equipment which was not paid the balance was not yours.
You must know you can not use the facilities or touch them without doing your job on duty for problem solving a pointed out already.

I am notifying you Xueyi Wu is accused of the same above to DISPUTE TRIBUNAL COURT filing on 1st December 2021.

Regards

Young soo Youn

* 9 NOV 2021 *

Freezer room
Condensing unit
Model : (RLTZ 150)
Running at 1.4kw @ -25 degree C.

Exclution:
* Crane   * Eva. X Fan 1
* Any council consents and permit.
* After hrs or weekend call out.

Note
Any additional work will be charge as extra.

INCLUSIONS:-
* Installation of all refrigeration units and e
* 404a Refrigerant.

8-2

→ * 12 Jan 2022 *

→ (AW54LZB1N) Condensing unit.
* Oil Seperator.
* Sigh Glass
* Drier
* HP/LP
2306 watts at -25 C Evaporating temp.

(Evaporator AL26) X Fan 2
2550 watts at -24 C evaporating temp.

Exclution:
* Any council consents and permit.
* After hrs or weekend call out.
* Main Power from switch board to out d

Note
* Any additional work will be charge as ex

→ * Balloon Quote *

* 9 NOV 2021 *

0 - Single Phase

Model	Compressor	Value
(RLTZ150)	CAJ2464Z	(34.5)
RLTZ200	FH2480Z	53.2

0 - Three Phase

Model	Compressor	Value
RLTZ300	TFH2511Z	74.2
RLTZ400	TAG2516Z	112.5

8-3

* 12 Jan 2022 *

Code	Model	Value
CK2213	BA16LMYB1	16.2
CK2214	BA18LZB1	18.0
CK2215	WJ22LZB1N	21.5
CK2216	WJ26LZB1N	26.8
CK2217	WJ31LZB1N	30.5
CK2218	AW43LMYB1N	43.1
CK2222	(AW54LZB1N)	(53.5)

8-4

* Accomplice *

anan．@frigie.com <anan．@frigie.com>
回复: anan．@frigie.com
收件人: xywu＠gmail.com
抄送: pete pen ＠gmail.com

Hello, Shirley, Please check the confirmation form my for the freezer. You will never get -18 C and if you mar compressor.

Regards

AANAN CHOHA

Chill36 ltd.

email : anan ＠frigie.com

Cell +642167

Ph +6492620

9-1

I received the second claim. Below is my submission.

* Defamation *

1. The main problem is Youngsoo installed the wrong condensing unit. His equipment selection and workmanship are incorrect. Whatever qualification or license he has, that is nothing to do with my requirement. My requirement is to get the freezer work properly. My freezer is not cooling that is the fact and he himself agreed that is not cooling when he said that now the controller has to be changed. he kept changing all the components one by one as he is not sure what is wrong. I attached the email communication of the supplier's proof.

11-1

Dear Sir/Madam   *** 100% Lie ***

In Youngsoo's claim dated 21/02/2022, he stated he can not admit Chill 360's report because there is no showing inspector license number & name on it. I made a phone call to tribunal and asked if tribunal could hire a specialist to do an onsite inspection. I was advised that tribunal does not do this. Therefore I hired White Refrigeration to do the inspection. Please find attached the report. → *** Manipulate Report ***

12-1

Manipulate Report

Freezer Room Condition Report

X&H Wu Ltd T/A
BP2Go Medowban Road, Remuera, Auckland 1072

On the 24th of May we attended to site at BP2Go Medowbank to assess the freezer room installation onsite. We have found several faults with the room and initial design as noted below. Please note that we were not privy to the initial design conversations, scope of works of contract and as such all issues noted are based on an industry standard design and installation.

Room size: 2600mm x 900mm x 2500mm
Evaporator: Patton Refrigeration BL20 (serial #TSU07U06002)
Condensing unit: Kirby AW43MHGB1N (serial #05F21 0200009)

Issues found on system:
Please note that these were the design/installation issues that were found onsite at the time of our site visit only and may not constitute a full list of issues.

1) Roof penetration.
   The roof penetration that the pipes go through is not sealed to industry standard and is a point that is likely to leak in the future. The penetration is wrapped in insulation tape which is likely to degrade in the weather. This penetration should be covered with either a goose neck style roof penetration cover or similar product to ensure long term water tightness.

2) Unit does not have a weather proof cover installed.
   The unit did not have a weather proof cover installed and a plastic bag has been wrapped around the electrical box of the unit. This is not a normal practice and a galvanised steel (or similar) weather proof cover should be installed to the unit. If this does not happen the system is likely to have a reduced life span due to water ingress to the electrical box and

12-2

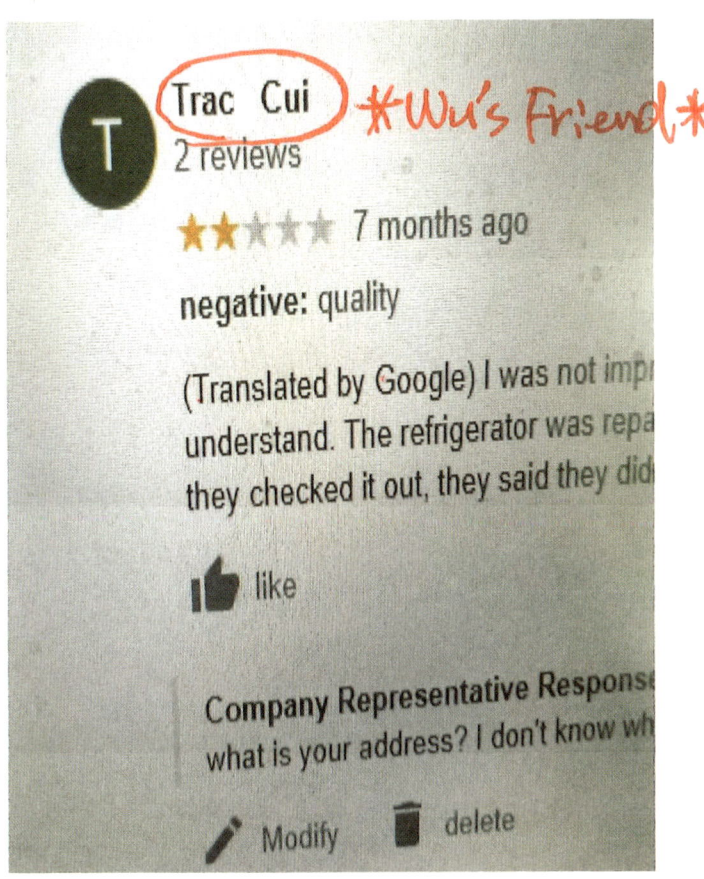

13-1

Wu's Friend

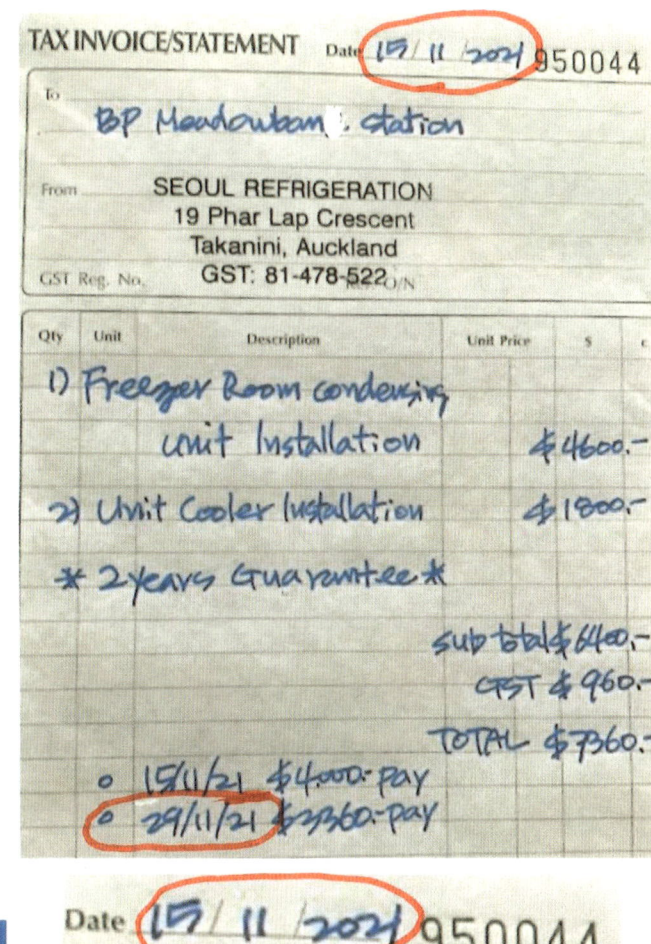

14-1

* promise day

23/11/21 actually *

Electrical Registration

Young Soo Youn

was registered as an **Electrical Service Technician** under the Electricity Act 1992 on 22 April 2004

Endorsement: This registration is limited to the maintenance and replacement of electrical appliances and fittings rated up to 460 volts including their disconnection from and reconnection to permanent wiring.

Registration No: EST 243006

N J J Sickels
Registrar

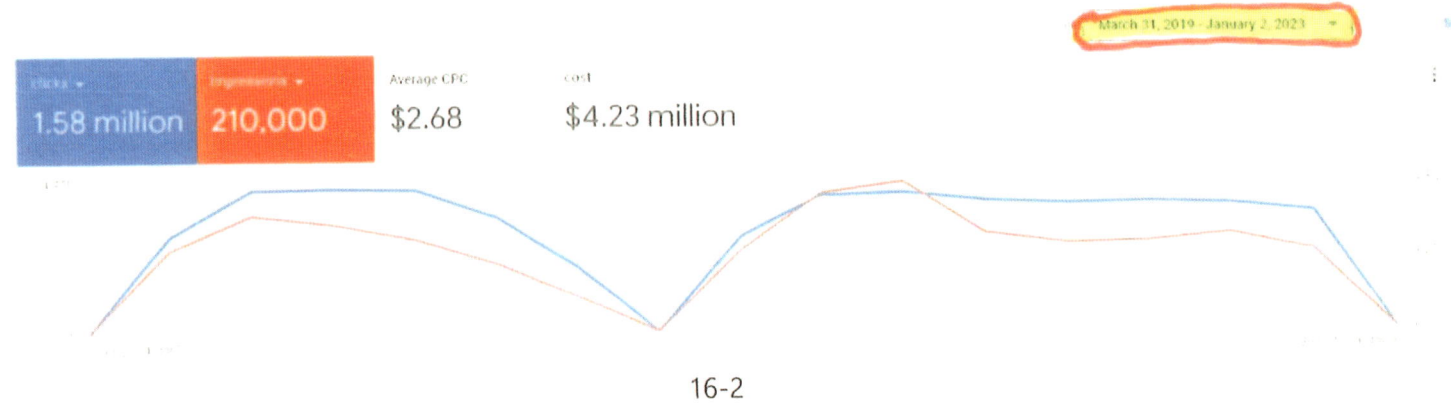

clicks: 1.58 million | impressions: 210,000 | Average CPC $2.68 | cost $4.23 million

March 31, 2019 - January 2, 2023

16-2

bidding statistics

45 months Average

March 31, 2019 - January 2, 2023

Show URL domain	impression share	overlap rate	high position percentage	Top of Page Rate	Top of page rate (abs rate value)
me	33.89%	—	—	73.2%	21.3%
fisherpaykel.com	20.49%	24.8%	43.27%	26.64%	16.59%
bunderscrack.co.nz	14.24%	20.2%	19.14%	65.17%	16.49%
jonesservices.co.nz	12.70%	17.5%	19.4%	74.57%	25.5%
justanswer.com	11.62%	15.41%	26.14%	53.6%	11.97%
axial.co.nz	10.30%	11.34%	26.95%	49.5%	10.65%
goappliances.co.nz	less than 10%	12.25%	21.5%	64.1%	14.2%
apexappliances.co.nz	less than 10%	11.74%	11.15%	31.41%	2.9%

Best One

16-3

Vividly Fixed Evidence

Case number: CIV-2021-055-000

Applicant: Youngsoo Youn

　　　　　　Seoul Refrigeration

Respondent: Xueyi Wu

　　　　　　BP Meadowban Station

Sir / Madam,

Allow me, I applicant Youngsoo Youn physically confirmed onsite directly as respondent Xue Wu's Freezer Room equipment was normally running on 11 March 2023 at 10pm.

(The justification for the on-site visit is based on photo evidence 7-2.)

It's time now consuming fighting allegations of both parties for a year and 4 months and 10 days after filing court must be terminated by this event.

1. I, applicant Youngsoo Youn, called up Wu's couple 2 days before finishing the installation work which they promised Bank transfer immediately after reaching -20°C. The reason of this act was because I confirmed the controller was out of order.

2. Respondent Wu threatened me with wrong technical information in collusion with unqualified person Anan for the purpose of welch the balance after breaking the promise. And she made a counter claim over 3 times amount of the balance with an exaggerated quotation in cooperation with Pete Refrigerator after awaking of the Court filing.

3. After Wu & conspirator Anan realized that their insistences were wrong Wu came

in contact with Whit Refrigeration and she submitted a manipulated absurd Report which the controller was not wrong this time to Court. At last, she had it reflected to Order of Dispute Tribunal approved 100% from Referee.

4. Is it possible indeed normal running without repairing or replacing new one of the broken controller? It is absolutely impossible !

Applicant: Youngsoo Youn

(During the on-site checking that day, I discovered something completely unexpected and surprising. The Condensing Unit had been 'replaced' with a new one that sparkled in the surrounding lighting.)

*(Its capacity is 2 levels higher, but the external size is the same with not even 1mm difference.
You can see why by looking at the letter 'I' sent to the referee.)*

Petition 2

Appellant   Youngsoo Youn

Respondent   Xue Wu

1. I, appellant Youngsoo Youn, directly submitted documents which were enclosed 'Petition of Appeal and Last Evidences' to Papakura District Court on 21st February 2023. And continuously submitted a 'Vividly Fixed Evidence' to Papakura District Court on 13th March 2023.
2. In the morning of 27th March 2023, after 34 days submitting the Petition of Appeal, 2 Police officers suddenly visited me my place. Purpose of the visit seemed to execute the court order on me.
3. I immediately let them see the 'Petition of Appeal' which was submitted to Court 34 days ago, and they went back after confirmation of it under appealing.

(It was difficult to understand the email at that point, 34 days later, but I just accepted it positively.)

4. I received an email in the early afternoon same day 27th March 2023 like attachment. (Attachment 1)

5. Following day 28th March 2023 at 10am I submitted another updated one which was partly erased the part in red squared line related to Referee on the petition of appeal from the original then.   (Attachments 5-1,

6. On 4th May 2023, I received an E-mail attachment like following attachment again after passing 37 days from the day of last submission.

*I interpret the emergency email I received from the court that day, my appeal, which was submitted twice on 21/02/2023 (1st time) and 28/03/2023 (2nd time), has been 'held' for a whopping 72 days. Now, I had no choice but to interpret it as the judge's decision that the appeal process could only proceed with the consent of the appellee Wu.

*If that's the case, then yes!

*Procrastinated 366 days with a small amount of money

*In the last hearing, she expressed hatred beyond disgust.

*With a simple commanding Order, the victim is instantly 'changed' into the assailant.

*The Order arrived 46 days after the deadline to prevent appeal.

*Even if the condensing unit was changed, where will the evidence go?

7. (The next day, 05/05/2023, while I was out briefly between 2 and 4 p.m., I found the execution letter left behind by the bailiff stuck to the concrete floor of the entrance, soaked in the rain.) (Attachment 7)
(deletion of parentheses)

I would appreciate if you let me know my fault or wrong doing for last 72 days like mentioned above 1 – 7.

1. I mentioned my imminent situation that I must close my business in the petition I submitted it to Court previously. And also I wanted all involved should be punished if there were offences.

2. If they were not realized their irrelevant acts which how much influenced to others as damage seriously, I will separately be preparing chances they could reflect by themselves for them thoroughly.

   Above two reasons are the facts I submit 'Petition of Appeal' and extremely want to see court's decision as soon as possible.

8th May 2023

Appellant

Youngsoo Youn

(To put things bluntly in points 1 and 2 above, I meant that all guilty people deserve to be punished, and if they are not punished, a way will be prepared for all of them to pay for their crimes.)

(So it took time.)

(That's why I had time to pay the money that day.) **(Page 80)**

(This case can be closed right away with just a smartphone photo that everyone has.)

*As is the case with all criminal cases, when the incident began, at the scene, at the scene, at the scene, at the evidence, if anyone just clicks once, this story will come to a clean end •

보낸 사람: Disputes Tribunal
보낸 날짜: 2023년 3월 27일 월요일 오후 3:43
받는 사람: seoulref@hotmail.com
제목: URGENT CIV-2021-055-000   Youn v Wu

Good Afternoon,

We are in receipt of your application attached for an appeal received on 1st March 2023. Unfortunately, we are unable to process the notice of appeal as you need to file application out of time. The Order of the Tribunal was issued on 02/12/2022.

A copy of the information for parties is enclosed.

Please kindly file the application for leave to file an appeal outside of the 20 working day period. There is a filing fee of $250 for that application. I have attached the form to be completed.

Please file Leave to appeal online using File and Pay - portal
https:/www.courtsof

Thee link to access File and pay is here: File and Pay — Courts (courtsof

Upon receipt of the filing fee, we will refer to the District Court Judge to consider the leave to file an appeal out of time.

Regards

        Deputy Registrar
        Ministry of Justice I Tahu o te Ture I

        Phone Number: 0800
        Email: disputes

        Website: www.

(ATT=1)

(Papakura Courts)
1. Dept (courts)
Papakura DC

```
--------FFTPOS------------*
MERCHANT    **********24319
TERMINAL              0001
28 Mar 23 10:34     CHEQUE
EFTPOS               SWIPE
CARD        ***********6924
RRN            001230210822
AUTHORISATION        611757
DPSTXNREF    0000000749538706
REFERENCE            005629
PURCHASE           NZD250.00
TOTAL              NZD250.00

      APPROVED

    PIN VERIFIED

*---------------------------*
    CUSTOMER COPY

    PLEASE RETAIN
    FOR YOUR RECORDS
```

S TRIBUNAL   CIV

                              Youngsoo Youn
                              ....
                              APPELLANT

                              Xue Wu
                              ....
                              RESPONDENT

APPLICATION FOR LEAVE TO FILE AN APPEAL OUTSIDE OF THE 20 WORKING DAY PERIOD ALLOWED AFTER THE HEARING.

CIV: 2021-055-000

REASON(S)

1. I, appellant Youngsoo Youn 'Order of the Tribunal' on 8th February 2023 (2 months and 6 days passed) by postal delivery.

2. Accordingly I, Youngsoo Youn, directly submitted 2 peeks of documents which were enclosed 'pitition of Appeal and Last Evidences' to Papakura District Court on 21st February 2023.

3. Continuously I directly submitted a 'Vividly Fixed Evidence' to Papakura District court on 13th March 2023.

4. I, Youngsoo Youn, am resubmitting the 'Petition of Appeal and Vividly Fixed Evidence' with Reasons of delay in this form.

Signed............
Name & contact Ph: Youngsoo Youn 021 624 963

Please lodge this form along with the Notice of Appeal

(ATT:5-1)

District Court

2 8 MAR 2023

PAPAKURA

I visited today, but you weren't home

Please call or text

Renee Hyde
Bailiff

urgently on

027 2506489

about ref.

justice.govt.nz

$5,432.33

From:

Business Current Account
SEOUL REFRIGERATION LTD
06-0177-0718   -00

To:

bp meadowban
01-0142-0245   -000

Payment date:
Mon 8 May 2023

[Save this payee]

This payment has been made immediately.

The Second Chapter

Criminal prosecution request letter sent to lawyer

- This letter was sent to lawyer by Korean, and translated literally in English after returning in refusal.

- From the overall content, content that was deemed unnecessary or inconvenient from the viewers' perspective was deleted.

- The indicated case number, person's name, company name are different from reality.

- The book page numbers in this chapter are incorrect because they have been re-edited.

Dear lawyer,

How have you been?

This is Youngsoo Youn from Seoul Refrigeration.

I am deeply grateful that I was able to resolve the problem smoothly thanks to the advise of you lawyer whenever I encountered difficulties.

This time, I am uploading this article with related materials attached to seek help from a lawyer for a 'serious issue' that is on a completely different level that before.

Firstly, I will explain the enclosed booklet titled 'The Facts & Lies and then Ignore', which was recently publiushed in Korea.
I filed this book in the Disputes Tribunal here as a simple case of 'claiming the balance of installation for failure to fulfill a promise'.
But the other party submitted incorrect claims, false documents, and fabricated quote of estimates to the court, and counterclaimed an amount that was more than three times the amount I claimed.

This is a 'Court Submission Document Record' that collects only the evidence documents submitted to the court and emails exchanged with the court in order to prove the other party's 'planned fraud' during the trial process that began.

However, the most important part to pay attention to in this record book is the fact that the Global Advertising Agency informed the court of the truth of the 'Organized killing of advertiser' committed against my company.
Therefore, let's review the 'truth' based on the contents of the book.
(In this book, relevant parts are marked as 'highlights' separately.)

    I.   Googl Ads Team

1. The day I opened a Googl Ads account was 31 March 2019.
   For the first five months of opening an account, I could always see my advertisement on the search top page normally, but after that, my advertisement had no 'principles and standards', such as moving across 4 to 5 pages or only showing my company name or phone number in large letters in the title of my advertisement. Incomprehensible advertisements continued to appear.
   Therefore, due to the nature of my business, which is 100% relying on the advertising, my income had no choice but to decrease by 30-40%.

2. While these abnormal advertisements continued, I raised the issue through the first tele-conference with the Ads team senior, and at this time, I received a reply from him saying, 'Please wait a little as it is an issue that needs to be raised at the headquarters.' A few months later, I contacted him again.

At the second tele-conference, I raised a strong issue and received a promise and pledge to publish it on the first page, but it was not kept. Afterwards, I sent several emails urging the company to fulfill its promise, but received no action of response. Several months later, after a tele-conference with another senior manager who had been replaced and the upper bid limit was significantly raised at his recommendation, things seemed to be returning to normal for only about 40 days.
One day, an order that crossed the line to 'replace the interpreter' was suddenly issued.

Then, incomprehensible behavior continued, such as the tyranny of fixing the placement of my advertisements from the previous 4-5 pages to 7-8 pages, as if in retaliation for the complaints filed so far.
In this way, the advertising team forces pushed my company out of the related service market compulsorily. It was a long-term, blatant expression of an organized movement to do this.

3. However, I learned why the 'G' advertising team continued to practice such 'unfair behavior' for a long time when I accidentally searched 'Bid statistics', which is updated and posted every day, one day, 2 years and 5 months after opening the account.

   Firstly, let's look at two cases.

*Case 1) Among the bidding statistics, this is the 'impression share' posted so that you can compare the performance of the related service section with other companies.
(Refer to book page 58 of 8.)

- If you look at the graph on the left, you can see a picture of my company floating high alone.
- If you look at the numbers in the chart on the right, it will be explained more clearly.

My company	57.87%	Top
Fisher & Paykel	18.36%	2nd
SAMSUNG	14.43%	3rd
LG	14.43%	4th

- Do you think these impossible and ridiculous statistics are actually correct?
- Can you imagine the unpleasant and confused feelings of advertisers or account managers who pay a considerable amount of advertising fee to receive these statistics, where performance is compared every day as if receiving aschool report?

*Case 2) This is the 'average market share for 45 months' in the related service section from the time I opened the account to the time of search.
(See book page 120, 16-3)

- Excluding North and West Auckland, Central, East and South Auckland, my company provides limited service while excluding places where parking is inconvenient or crowded, such as CBD, shopping malls, Apts, etc., and has an average market share of 33.89% Top over the past 45 months.

- Fishe & Payke, a global home appliance manufacturer with a nationwide unlimited service network, ranked second with an average market share of 20.49% during the same period (and that was a whopping 13.4% difference, not 1-2%).
  Do you understand what criteria, what numbers, and how they were calculated so that these statistics are updated and published every day?

5. The previous advertising team's 'killing advertisers' project It seems clear that the main reason for the continuation of 'absurd statistics' is the purpose of so-called 'ostracizing' my company in the 'related industry'.
   This is because, even before I was convinced to discover the 'statistics in question,' I was experiencing great complaints about blatant 'checks and cold treatment' from my main clients, major companies that provide services and parts, major home appliances, manufacturers, and parts processing departments.

6. Because of such things that bothered me, I was feeling half-motivated to even do the work I enjoyed as an extension of what I had done my whole life, and that is when I came across the 'statistic in question.' In such a situation, there was no reason to continue the business while enduring increasing losses due to their tricks.
   Therefore, I have decided to close our business as of 31 March 2022, three years after my bad relationship with Googl.
   When I decided to 'voluntarily close down the business', it was a month and a half before I encountered 'another bad relationship' that I was inevitably bound to encounter due to Googl.

7. This 'bad encounter' eventually led to a legal battle, and during the ensuing trial, the refrigeration companies that were influenced by the previous 'bullying' part joined the side of my opponent, the 'suspected fraudster', and manipulated the documents to be submitted to the court.
   I think it had a big impact in completely overturning the court decision.
   Therefore, my 'voluntary closure of business' had to be postponed until now, about two years later.

8. Last July, I made a booklet identical to the enclosed book, written only in English, and sent it to Googl headquarters along with the quotation I received from the publisher. The reason for sending it was that there were plans to publish this book, so everything had to be normalized now. Here, everything refers to the situation in which not only the Ads team but also the project team participated in the 'killing advertisers'

project in addition to what was promised, which meant that even the part they knew very well had to be restored to its original state.
* But they did what they always do: they ignored it.

9. About a month ago, I sent a booklet published in Korea, same identical to the enclosed book, to Googl headquarters. (Att. 9-1)

The reason why I sent a book with the same English contents again as in July of last year was in the hope that this time I would be able to recover some of the self-esteem that had been unilaterally ignored and trampled upon over the past five years. However, they made no move or reaction, as if they were laughing at and questioning the contents, saying, 'you wanted it published by yourself, why do you keep sending it?'

** This very part is the whole reason why I had no choice but to find a lawyer. **

Now, I will postpone the matter of asking the lawyer for help for a moment and explain 'the other issue', which is inevitably connected to the previous Googl Ads team issue, but it is a separate case.

24. 3. 4. 오후 2:29   (Att.9-1)   Tracking | NZ Post

"The Facts & Lies and then Ignore, Book 출판 예고

The latest NZ Post app is available now! Download it today for better parcel visibility, and easy access to your favourite NZ Post tools.

To Google 1st. 24 July 2023 04:30 PM. (Sent) (Notice of scheduled publication) (출판 예정 통보)
2nd. 15 February 2024 11:14 AM. (출판 완료 통보) (Notice of completion of publication)

Dismiss   Learn more

Enter your tracking number here   [Track]

☐ Select all (1)   Filter by

☐ EP459424442NZ   Parcel options ⋮

✓ **Delivery Complete**
11:04am, 22 February 2024
Your item has been delivered and was signed for by "D WILLIAMS"

● **Attempted delivery**
10:23am, 22 February 2024

● **Ready for collection**
10:23am, 22 February 2024

● **At local/regional depot**
10:22am, 22 February 2024

● **Released for delivery**
10:51am, 21 February 2024, Los Angeles, United States

● **International arrival**
02:26pm, 17 February 2024, Los Angeles, United States

● **Held for clearance**
02:26pm, 17 February 2024, Los Angeles, United States

● **With border agency**
02:26pm, 17 February 2024, Los Angeles, United States

● **International departure**
08:44am, 16 February 2024, Auckland, New Zealand

● **Processed at outbound depot**
07:27am, 16 February 2024, Auckland, New Zealand

● **Picked up/Collected**

II. Xue Wu

1. The 'bad relationship' between me and the gas(fuel) station owner named Xue Wu started when, due to the 'G' advertising team not keeping their promise, no orders came in even during the peak season, so I had to do something that I would normally 'with a flat refusal'. It had begun.

2. From the beginning, she conspired with her boyfriend, an HVAC salesman similar to refrigeration, to deliberately approach me to complete the refrigeration facility at her gas station, which had not been used from the gas station long since and it was also seriously broken and had been idle for a long time, without spending any money by herself.

3. By the time I found out her intentions, I had already started the work, and in order to escape from her clutches, she was an innately bad person who immediately broke the promise to pay the balance, which I had lured her with an extra amount of money two days before the work was completed.

4. So I ended up filing with the Disputes Tribunal. Then, she submitted documents to the court requesting a counterclaim of more that three times the amount she had claimed, based on a false report written by her unqualified boyfriend and a fabricated estimate from a refrigeration company arranged by him.

5. The second and final hearing of the small claims dispute trial was held one year and one day after filing. In the meantime, I submitted her 'documents proving the fraud charges' to the court four times.

6. However, the small claims dispute trial continued to fail, including on the last hearing day, and 10 months and 2 days after that date, the court approved my 'intention to give up the appeal' (Attachment 6-1) and ended my relationship with her. The 'Disputes Tribunal' has been concluded.

7. I collected 'detailed circumstantial evidence' regarding the previous 'crippling' and asked a lawyer to accept it (see attachment), but it was rejected.
It's all contained in the published book right from the beginning until it was rejected.
In the book, the contents of the 'letter to the lawyer' are briefly introduced through the Korean 'author's commentary', but in the separate booklet I am sending to the lawyer today, you will be able to fully understand the 'true nature of the lameness'.

8. However, paradoxically, if there had not been 'such a failure', the Googl Ads team's 'unfair acts' would have ended with one company closing down and quietly disappearing, and Xue Wu and her ring group would have been fine with their unfair acts in the 'civil trial' as well, so like that they must have looked down on the law.

9. If you look at the preface of the enclosed 'The Facts & Lies and then Ignore booklet, you will see why I wrote this book.
   For what purpose I was it used?
   So what am I going to do?

   *The answer is that I don't want anything.

   *I wrote the book because this was the only way to rid myself of dishonor.

   *If Goog had seen this published book I sent and placed an ad for just one day to fulfill a promise made four years ago and restore my credit rating, I would have closed down my business and retired from that day.

   *Xue Wu and her ring have also long since be erased from my memory.

   ** Now I desperately need help from you Lawyer. **

(Att.6-1)

보낸 사람: Auckland_Civil_CMT
보낸 날짜: 2023년 10월 4일 수요일 오전 11:46
받는 사람: 윤 영수
제목: RE: CIV-2023-055-000   Youn v Wu

Good morning Youngsoo,

Thank you for your email and filing the completed Notice of Discontinuance.

I have processed this and the above matter is now Closed in the District Court. The Appeal Conference scheduled for the 19 October 2023 is vacated and the decision from the Disputes Tribunal stands.

Many thanks,

Kind Regards I Naku noa na

Court Registry Officer I Civil Team
Ministry of Justice I Tahu o te Ture I Auckland District Court
69 Albert Street I Private Bag 92191 I Auckland 1142I
P: 0800 268 787 I E: Auckland_Civil_CMT@justice.govt.nz
Website:www.justice.govt.nz

From: 윤 영수 <seoulref@hotmail.com>
Sent: Wednesday, 4 October 2023 11:03 am
To: Auckland_Civil_CMT <Auckland_Civil_CMT@justice.govt.nz>
Subject: RE: CIV-2023-055-000   Youn v Wu

Dear Sir/Madam

I attached the file that Resubmitted.
Thanks

Kind regards
Youngsoo Youn

보낸 사람: Auckland_Civil_CMT
보낸 날짜: 2023년 10월 3일 화요일 오전 10:29
받는 사람: 윤 영수
제목: RE: CIV-2023-055-000   Youn v Wu

* Help from You Lawyer *

1. Please review whether criminal charges can be filed against the Google Ads team.

2. As a separate matter, please consider whether criminal charges can be filed against Xue Wu and her associates.

3. If it is determined that prosecution is possible as a result of reviewing both 1 and 2 above,

4. I would like to form a strong team of civil and criminal lawyers centered on lawyers, including a law firm that can compete against the powerful Google, which has a legal team.

5. I do not want even $1 in monetary compensation for both 1 and 2 above.

6. Therefore, I think the only way to cover court costs is to file a separate civil lawsuit.

7. As I who is completely unfamiliar with the law, it seems clear that they do not want to drag on this shameful 'sensitive issue' committed by their Ads team for long. It may be presumptuous, but I think there would be a way to file a lawsuit by setting sufficient legal fees in advance.

8. I have no further supporting materials other than the attached documents submitted along with the two booklets 1 and 2 above.

9. Submitted brochures and attached documents will be provided upon your request.

I look forward to seeing you soon.

Client Youngsoo Youn on 22 March 2024

Dear Lawyer,

Hello

I believe that by now you are carefully reviewing the evidence I sent you last week.

This week, I decided that it would be helpful for you lawyer in your review to analyze and inform the cause of all these incidents, so I picked up the pen.

In addition, the Googl Ads team, which opened the account 5 years ago, and the profile team, which started intervening 2 years ago, will attach evidence of the results achieved so far and send it to you by email.

1. Cause

There are three ways in which my business 'Service Type' is different from other companies.

1) Fridge Freezer Repair Only
2) No charge, No Fix
3) Telephone estimate & Site solve

*Services other than those shown in advertisements

1) 1 year free after-service for same part failure
2) 1 Free service for two problems simultaneously happened
3) If fixation is not possible even if other parts are broken, 1/2 refund within 3 months

*All of the above are services that are impossible for a 'company that must pursue profit'.

*This service is only available to 'one-person company that does not pursue profit.'

2. Googl's 'Easy malicious judgment' that it would disappear within 2-3 months at most if it just blocks the source of income rather than the 'difficult practical judgment' of creating a program suitable for the above 'Service type' is the 'unimaginable deformed statistic'.
It is believed that this has become the starting point that will inevitably continue for five years.

3. Xue Wu, relayed by Googl, was the person who escalated the incident to this point by colluding with her boyfriend, not her husband, from the beginning, using the 'No charge No Fix' section above.

4. The circumstances that led to the involvement of the Googl profile team were that Trac Cu who is believed to be a friend of Xue Wu, posted a false malicious comment in the business review managed by the team, combined with three malicious comments that had not been of interest to date.
I asked the team to delete the '4 malicious comments' but they finally informed me that they were 'rejecting the deletion request' after long time hampered and I confirmed that the profile team, following the Ads team, is also intervening.
(See book page 108, paragraph 13)

Below is about 'Trac Cu who posted false bad comments.

Trac Cu

2 years ago

Wasn't impressed the work, very poor English and hard to understand. Fixed the fridge but after few months same issue happened and came over checked and said that don't know what is the problem.
Wouldn't recommend.

Company representative response (Owner's reply)

What is your address? I don't know who you are? I never did like that!

* It is said that 33 pages (Korean) of the book will be omitted from the 14-page manuscript. Below is the 'explanation of evidence' part of the omitted evidence submitted to the court regarding the malicious comment posted by Trac Cu two years ago.

In the end, one thing (*Attachment 8) my Business Review on last 11th May 2022

I am 20 years experienced Qualified Technician. This incident should never happened to me. It is seemed that this Review which WU had her friend Cui ordered to be used when take a chance in this Hearing. Ex) "I never promised to pay the balance immediately.", "His English ability was very poor, so I never the words...etc."

*I think it is clear that the 'Very poor English' part of 'Trac Cu 's fake malicious comment is at the center of all the issues I am experiencing as a first-generation immigrant.
This problem is that not only Referee, Googl , and Xue Wu, but also everyone who has spoken or spoken to me on the phone will recognize me as 'impaired in English expression' when there is a conflict of interest, and will be 'armed' and 'unresponsive' even if they attack me unconditionally. They all believe that they brought the current 'helpless situation' upon themselves by making a mistake and making a planless attack.

5. Service industry is an industry that is responsible for meeting customer needs in exchange for a fee.

However, as you can see from my business type, my service is structured so that no malicious comments can be posted. Therefore, the people who posted malicious comments on my service are fake like the previous 'Cui', or they were unfriendly when talking on the phone, or they came on a business trip and did not provide service and just left, etc.
They distorted the facts and lied about the hurtful situation that occurred outside of the service. They are making up comments and leaving malicious comments. In this case, too, it can be seen that there are malicious comments based on the content of the last sentence of number 4.

6. If the Googl profile team had accepted my deletion request two years ago, it is clear that I would have maintained my highest credit rating of 5 points.

The reason is that not only have there been no malicious comments in the previous three years, but I have never met anyone in the past 20 years who did not appreciate the service I provided, except for one person. That one time it was 'Xue Wu'.

7. I think it is clear that people who leave malicious comments muster up the courage to do bad things after seeing the malicious comments posted first.

Just two years ago, after the request for deletion of the picture was rejected, malicious comments began to follow immediately, and as more than 10 malicious comments continued over the past two years, my business credit rating finally fell to 3 points.
Immediately after that, my monthly sales suddenly dropped by 31%, from $4,738.00 in average sales for the previous three months to $3,260.00 in March.

8. I am sure that this miserable feeling is what Googl wanted from the beginning.

The reason is that the Ads team was able to prove that by posting 'absurd statistics' on the related service market every day, I was 'ostracized' by related companies, and then the profile team rejected the request for deletion, causing me to be shunned by customers.

9. Let's look at the latest bidding statistics, which are no different from the past.

Display URL domain	impression share	Top of page coverage
me	29.35%	54.24%
fisherpaykel.com	23.38%	89.36%
sbappliance.co.nz	16.42%	87.88%
directair.nz	12.94%	92.31%
builderscrack.co.nz	10.95%	72.73%
essentialair.co.nz	less than 10%	76.47%

(5 days ago — March 28, 2024)

* Why does my top of page coverage needs to be 54.24%?
* Why does my Ad the top even though it is 54.24% in Display URL domain?
* Whether it's 54.24% or 70-80%, it's always on top, but why has it become a daily occurrence that my paid advertisement is located below the free advertisement of Dryer Repair Service?
* It cannot be denied that this is an irony and mystery that has been repeated countless times over the past 4 years and 7 months.

10. The following are details of 'two cases of malicious comments' that caused my business credit rating to drop to 3 points and sales to drop by more than 30% overnight.
I will explain in detail the evil deeds of these trash people with evidence.

< Instance 1 >

Jis Thoma Vincen

3 weeks ago

I called guy to fix my fridge because it wasn't cooling enough. He came twice (he couldn't fix it the first time) to fix it and charged us 280$ just to put that black double-sided tape to keep the damper open. Now it is freezing everything in the fridge because it can't close automatically. Should have replaced the damper.
I ordered a new one and replaced it myself for 65$.
I am editing this with a photo of what the technician did. It was the original problem. Doing something in the freezer when it's clearly a problem with the damper shows how fraud this guy is. Please be very careful when you deal with this guy.

Company representative response (Owner's reply)

Hey Thoma !

First day, I solved a big problem that occurred more than 80% of the case with the same model of Refrigerator of the same brand after getting $280.00.
Second day, after I confirmed a broken damper and took a measure of it's treatment. Even though it was clearly different problem I did it for free without receiving any money.

And, double-sided tape? and Freezing everything?
One is wrong and the other is a lie.
Why do you distort the facts and even lie, making the technician who solved the problem an fraudster?

For your information, anyone who posts malicious comments about my service is 100% human trash. Find out why in the owner's reply.
I hope you deeply reflect on my advice.

+ Jis Thoma Vincen +

* This malicious commenter has been telling lies from the beginning.
* He did not call me, but the person who called was a woman.
* On the first day It's not that I couldn't fix it , but the work was completed perfectly that day. A calling woman who had been watching the work seemed to think $280 was cheap compared to the amount of work, so she followed me out to the front door after finishing the work and said she would deposit the money immediately. She thanked me twice repeatedly.

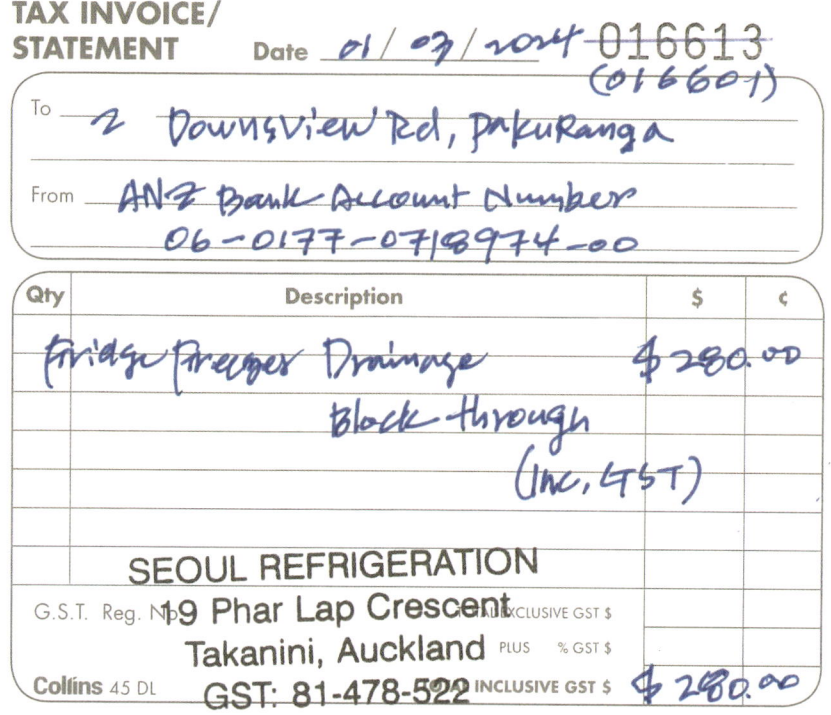

* On the second day I saw him for the first time, and although it was something very unusual and clearly different, it was a permanent measure, not a temporary measure, and the service was provided free of charge without additional charge.
* He lied saying like, "Now it is freezing everything."
  The reason is that the tape I installed permanently is a functional tape of a thickness that has been verified through numerous tests and measurements to ensure that the high cold temperature no longer falls below 0°C .
* He lied and distorted it as if he solved the problem that the technician couldn't.
* They took $280 without fixing it on the first day?
  Spend $65.00 to completely fix it yourself?
  He's a scammer, be careful?
* Please also take action on Thomas   that Xue Wu, who posted a malicious comment by immediately criticizing the specialist me who has been doing the same thing here everyday for 22 years as a fraudster, can go where she needs to go.

< Instance 2 >

Seoul Refrigeration
3.9

Kirte Meht

1 month ago

DO NOT GET ANYTHING DONE THROUGH THIS GUY!!! FIRSTLY HE IS EXTREMELY RUDE WHILE TALKING, HE DEMANDED ON THE SPOT MONEY $1700 FOR A PART TO BE REPLACED IN OUR FRIDGE WITHOUT MAKING PROPER CONSULTATION NOR GIVING ANY IDEAS TO WHAT THE FAULT IS. SECONDLY ONE WEEK LATER THE PART HE REPLACED FAILED AND FRIDGE STOPPED WORKING. WHEN I CALLED HIM TO ASK HIM TO COME AND SEE WHAT IS GOING ON HE STARTED SHOUTING IN SOME LANGUAGE THAT NO ONE UNDERSTANDS. HE THEN HUNG UP AND DOESN'T RESPOND TO ANY MAESSAGES!!!! BE ABSOLUTELY AWARE OF THIS PERSON RIPPING PEOPLE OFF... I AM GOING TO COMMERCE COMMISSION NOW TO TAKE THIS UP FURTHER

Company representative response (Owner's reply)

Hey Kirte !

I've never seen nor known you.
You don't know about the work at all.
That's wholly a wrong story.
You were such a trash person that you threat me
to call the police from the first phone call.

Disputes Tribunal

CIV: 2024-094
Date Received: 13/02/2024
Courthouse: Auckland District Court
Filed by: Applicant

Form 1: Claims Form

Part 1: Applicant	
Organisation's name:	Roop Takeways Limited
Organisation's contact:	Kirtes Meht.
Physical address	
Floor/Building:	
Street or road (number and name):	SHOP 6 / 48 RICHARDSON ROAD
Rural delivery number:	
Suburb:	MOUNT ROSKILL
City, town or district:	AUCKLAND
State:	
Postcode:	1041
Postal address (if different from physical address)	
Floor/Building:	
Street or road\PO Box,Bag or DX:	70 SANDRINGHAM ROAD
Rural delivery number:	
Suburb:	WESLEY
City, town or district:	AUCKLAND
State:	
Postcode:	1041
Contact Details:	
Daytime contact phone number:	
Mobile telephone number:	[64][21] 8889
Email address:	roo @roo co.nz

Part 4: Details of dispute	
Is this a new claim or a counter claim:	New Claim
Counter claim CIV number:	
Amount asked to be awarded:	$5,500.00

What does the applicant claim happened?

Hello team,

Young (or similar) from Seoul Refrigeration was called to check on an issue with the fridge on January 25, 2024. Upon arrival, he apparently decided that the fault was in the compressor and that he would need to replace it. My parents (who are also the directors of the business) agreed to have it replaced. Before I could get to know about this, the compressor was replaced, and an invoice was generated for $1700.00 (which he demanded an immediate on-the-spot payment). Once I had received this information and the invoice, I called to ask what led him to replace the compressor (considering my parents do not speak English and they may not know). This is the question I asked him, as I believed that if there was anything that was not age- or normal wear-related, I may be able to get insurance to look into it. However, he started shouting at me, asking for immediate payment, and he also stormed into the store, asking for payment. Unfortunately, I was not in store at the time, and my parents, who are 70 or older, decided that they did not want to make this man unhappy, and for that, they should pay him. Here the payment was made, he made a few days of follow-up trips, and he kept on fixing something without talking to anyone or telling anyone what he was doing. Given that my parents didn't want much of the hassle, they let him fix what they thought could be part of the routine fix after the compressor was replaced.

Now, two weeks later, on February 13, 2024, the fridge stopped working completely all of a sudden. We made a contact back to Seoul Refrigeration to see why this could be. Young came in to promptly check the fridge and told my parents that we would need to use the hair dryer to dry ice from the compressor every second day.

I found this very unusual, as we have had this fridge new for over 6 years and have never had to do this. I tried calling him to speak to him. Young refused to talk to me in spite of me repeatedly telling him that I am one of the owners of the takeaways and i needed to know (exactly the same way that I spoke with him in the first instance) why we needed to do this. He told us that its not his problem and he didn't want to know. He will not respond to my text email or answer my calls.

Now, $1700 later, we are sitting with a problem that I will need to get fixed by someone else. I lost a lot of my productions as I was unable to store it anywhere. Also, I am facing the need to run around and find a way for me to bring this person or company to justice and own up to their mistake.

I will look forward to hearing back from you.

regards,
Kirte Meht
02188899

Additional docs:

　　WhatsApp Image 2024-02-13 at 15.12.21.jpeg

Additional documents to file separately with the court: No

==Ladies and Gentleman who know Roo   Vegetarian Takeaway!==

I am a Qualified Technician who has been doing Refrigerator Repair Service here in Auckland for 22 years.

I have visited Roo   shop in Mount Roskil and have had them serviced several times before. I didn't know it at the time, but I learned now that the old shop owner was a very bad person.

1. Last January, I decided to exchange the condenser fan including the comp., which was so covered in oil that the compressor inevitably died, and she promised to pay $1,700. After the work was completed, she said it would be paid twice and I said okay, but the next day, a man whom I had never heard or seen on the phone called 'Roo   and told me that if I wrote a report, he would submit it to the insurance company and pay me $1,700 with the company's money. After some arguing, I said I would go to the shop right away and went there to complain and received $1,700.

2. That day, I discovered a fundamental and structural problem at the bottom of the cooling box that had not occurred because the temperature inside the chiller could not maintain the appropriate temperature, and explained the situation in detail to her youngest son to make him understand. The next day, I went to the shop and performed additional technical work free of charge to prevent the problem from occurring frequently.
The work is completely separate matter. The reason why I did the job for nothing was because her husband had expressed to me an apology on his son's bad action had done the day before. (Even though he was old, I had never seen that here, dedicating himself to his family by sweating all day in front of a hot oven, doing the dangerous and difficult job of frying ingredients in oil.)
She should be grateful that the problem that her youngest son had to do at least once every 2-3 days was able to be used without a problem for two weeks because I gave it to him for free.

3. Two weeks later, when the problem arose again, she called me with the whole family, hoping to solve the problem for free this time again. The reason I knew about her 'bad intentions' was because her younger son who knew the problem very well. Pretending not to know about the problem as soon as he saw me and told 'nonsense'. So I told him how to solve the problem, and then someone was relaying what I said to several people in the kitchen, and I left the shop.

4. Then, less than 1 hour later, the man who scammed me not to pay money before threatened me on the phone, saying, "If you don't come to the shop

right away, I'll call the police," and I hang up. And he sent me a threatening text message that If I do not reply within 30 minutes he will be taking some action continuously.

5. The next day, I saw her eldest son's malicious comment on Googl Business Review. The malicious comment can be seen in Seoul Refrigeration Review. Just find 'Kirte Meht and 'Owner's Reply'. For your information, all people who leave malicious comments to me are 'human trash'. The answer is in 'Owner's Reply'.

6. I sent the Repair Report three days later as promised. In that report, I made it clear that "I am not responsible for the part you are taking issue with." I also kindly explained him maintenance methods to solve the problem.

7. When I arrived a few days ago after being away from home for personal reasons, I saw a document filed against me by Roo takeaway at the 'Distribute Tribunal'. When I looked at the contents, they charged me a whopping $5,500.00 with all sorts of lies. At this level, there would never be a robbery like this.

8. Ladies and gentlemen, I don't know how good at Roo is making delicious food, but I would like to inform you that the owner of Roo and her son are 'human trash'.

Hello!

'Notice to your customers' previously posted is to inform you in advance of an article posted by 'Roo Vegetarian' in Business Review on 1 April 2024.
If you do not want this review to be posted, you must
1) withdraw this case filed with 'Distribute Tribunal' before the end of this month, and
2) restore the malicious comment your son posted.

Way to solve out; 1) You can send proo of 'withdrawal' to my email address.
2) Anyone with and IP address can simply review 'Good Service' in my Business Review and give it 5 stars.

If you do not resolve these two issues by the end of this month,
I will immediately post this review in the morning of 1st April 2024,
and file a counter claim to the court the correspondence texts and evidence exchanged amongst you and your son and me.

In my counter claim, your son who does not know the contents and has no contact with me, will request to be taken out.
I will also apply for an interpreter. You and I must meet at the hearing in a month's time on 1st of May.

I hope something unfortunate like that doesn't happen.

+ Kirtes Meht +

* Kirtes Meht , like Thoma Vincen is a human trash who dropped my business credit rating to 3 points by posting lies and malicious comments a few days apart about a month ago, reducing my sales by more than 30% in a day.

* Kirtes Meht is someone I have never met, but needless to say. Every time he opened his mouth, it was a blackmail threat, and every text I received was also a blackmail threat.

* He lies even in malicious comments and lies in all his claims at the Disputes Tribunal.

* When they first tried to give me the $1,700.00, I went to the shop and asked, "What is your poor son doing?" When I asked him, he said "Sherry," but I didn't know what "Sherry" does.

* Anyway, following the malicious comments, we have filed with the Disputes Tribunal, so please allow us to file criminal charges against Kirte .
Please take a look at the story I want to tell you, as it is all contained in the 'Message to Roo . Customers' on the previous page.

* For reference, even though the deadline to upload to Review has passed 4 days, there has been no response, so it appears that they are thinking that they will not lose anything by going to the end of DT. Just like Xue Wu was a huge successful woman! *

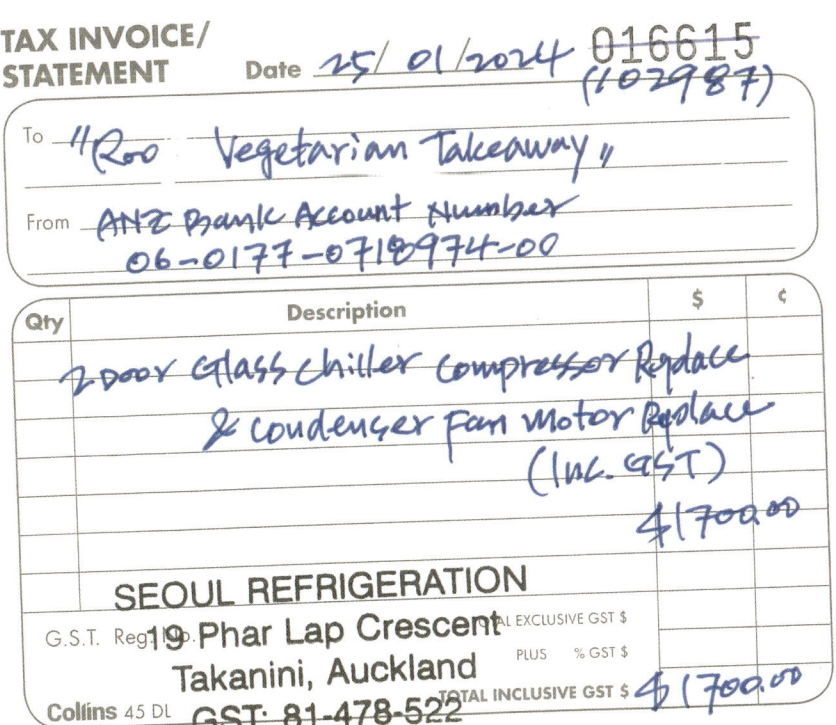

11. Last report received from Google

Business Profile report for 53 interactions* last month

This is the result of comparing March 2024 performance of Seoul Refrigeration, located at 19 Phar Lap Crescent Takanini, AUCKLAND 2112, with last month's performance.

[View full report]

Performance at a glance

- 📞 **10** call −61%
- 💬 **0** message
- ◆ **28** User who asked for location −6%
- 🖱 **15** Visit a website from your profile −28%
- 👁 **405** Profile View −19%
- 🔍 **21** search

*An interaction is considered when a customer calls, sends a message, makes a reservation, goes to your website, or requests directions in their business profile.

Popular searches

* The above is the final report that announces the completion of the 'Devil's Project' that Google has been longing for.

* Now my business can no longer exist.
 The r business that customers do not call Seoul Refrigeration any more.

Dear Lawyer,

Now, let me conclude.

It all happened because Google didn't keep its promises.

Even so, this situation would never have come if they had kept their promise for just one day when I sent the last published booklet.

Now, Google will definitely have to pay for the sin of trampling on even the immigrant life that they endured for over 22 years with nothing but pride.

From now on, I think it is your work.

I wish you good luck.

4 April 2024

Client   Youngsoo Youn

Epilogue

Everything in world begins through promise, and ends in keeping the promise.

Types of promises could be classified to following several ways in general.

The promise made by himself or herself, promise made by spouse, promise made by family, promise made by others and promise made by workplace.

Any promise must be kept. Anyone must get a consent from the other party even though any situation were happened.

Even the promise to himself or herself must be agreed by one's conscience.

Breaking promise without consent is just like to deceive one's conscience.

This story is about people who are deceiving their conscience.

Those who broke the promises would be hurt with heavy burden to spouse, family, colleagues and seniors in their workplace.

They all had reasons of deceiving their conscience because they were thoroughly to ignore the other party without exception.

This story is conceived by forming a Trinity of promise, conscience and ignorance.

The day a new life born in the near future, an old life will be vanished to backstage quietly.